THE
HEART
OF THE
SOUL

Emotional Awareness

GARY ZUKAV
AND
LINDA FRANCIS

SIMON & SCHUSTER SOURCE

New York   London   Toronto   Sydney   Singapore

SIMON & SCHUSTER SOURCE
1230 Avenue of the Americas
New York, New York 10020

Manufactured in the United States of America

Designed by Lisa Chovnick
Illustrations © 2002 Melanie Marder Parks

3   5   7   9   10   8   6   4

Library of Congress Cataloging-in-Publication Data is available.

ISBN   0-7432-0567-7

We dedicate this book to our human family
with joy, appreciation and love.

Acknowledgments

We are grateful to our cofounders of Genesis: The Foundation for the Universal Human, who have assisted and encouraged us in our exploration of emotional awareness. We are grateful to Oprah Winfrey, Jeffrey Jacobs, and Hollye Jacobs for their helpful suggestions and loving support. We are also grateful to Neale Donald Walsch for inspiring the perfect title; Fred Hills, our editor, for his masterful guidance; and Melanie Parks for her beautiful illustrations.

Contents

Welcome

OUR ADOPTED SIOUX UNCLE ONCE TOLD ME, "Nephew, the longest journey that you will make in your life is from your head to your heart," gently touching his forehead and then his chest.

Linda Francis, my spiritual partner, and I are still on that journey, and so are you. Everyone is on it. The journey into the heart is our future and our only way of creating a future. It is movement toward wholeness, integrity, and compassion. It is the healing each of us longs for, and the healing that each of us must accomplish if we are to move forward into our fullest potential.

Learning to experience emotions is one of the most difficult tasks that can be undertaken. Many people do not know that they are angry, even when rage flows through them like a river. Some do not know that they are grieving, even when sorrow is the only sun that rises for them in the morning. Most people think of themselves as experiencing emotions only when powerfully emotional currents erupt through their lives, disturbing routines devoted to activities, accomplishments, or survival.

Emotional awareness—becoming aware of everything that you are feeling at every moment—is very difficult because we experience so much pain each moment. Becoming aware of our emotions means becoming aware of pain. It is challenging, difficult, and unpleasant. It is also more rewarding than most of us can imagine. That is because most of us cannot imagine a life free from compulsions, fixations, obsessions, and addictions, in which we act with an empowered heart and are free of attachment to the outcome.

The alternative to becoming aware of your emotions is to continue masking the pain that you experience. When you do, your pain emerges in unexpected ways—distorting your behavior, changing your words, shaping your perceptions, and creating consequences that are as unwanted as they are difficult.

This alternative no longer works. Our species is undergoing an unprecedented transformation. Its consciousness is changing. Its perceptions are changing. Its values and goals are also changing. Individual by individual, old aspirations are being replaced by new. Comfort and influence are no longer goals that inspire, even those who live in poverty. The new goal is spiritual development. An awareness is emerging in millions of individuals that we are more than bodies and minds, more than enzymes and molecules, and that each of us is more than a temporary presence in the Universe.

This awareness is transforming the human experience. As it does, the determination to explore every aspect of consciousness, and to cultivate those that contribute the most to Life, is replacing the desire to bury painful emotions. This requires emotional awareness.

I am an author by choice, inclination, and aptitude. I love language. I love the rhythm and flow of words and sentences as they clothe ideas and give them expression. I love the challenge of writing without ambiguity, even though I know that is impossible. I know the slipperiness of language, and the delight of it. I know the limitations of my native language, and I honor the capabilities of other languages to shape thought and experience differently. I was born to know and use language. I am a fish and concept is my water.

Shortly after I met Linda eight years ago she told me, "Beloved, language is my second language." Now we have cocreated a book together. Linda's language is relationship. She excels at empathic communication—she is sensitive to others and she often knows what they feel. She swims confidently in a sea of emotion. Her challenge is articulate expression. Mine is consciousness of emotion. Both of us strive to create authentic power in our own lives—the alignment of the personality with the soul.

This is the context in which we cocreated this book. In her moments of clarity, Linda's expression is powerful. Her words are appropriate. Her meaning is unmistakable. Her expression is flawless. In my moments of sensitivity, emotions fill my awareness. I cherish people. I feel what they feel as well as what I feel. I love Life.

Linda and I have the same combination of qualities within us that you do—some that are strong and well-developed, and some that are yet to be developed. We have each drawn on our strengths in the cocreation of this book. I wrote the text, and Linda added dimensions to the text that I did not consider.

All of my books in the past have been solely (and souly) text—words, sentences, paragraphs, and chapters. This book is much more. It includes illustrations, diagrams, empowering thoughts, and, most important, authentic power practices. Authentic power is the alignment of your personality with your soul. You must become aware of what you are feeling in order to create authentic power. These practices are designed to help you do that.

A central practice in this book is a scan of what you are experiencing in your body. It is easy to understand how to do this and why it is important. However, to actually observe your emotions moment by moment will take commitment and effort on your part, no matter how experienced you are with practices.

Some people easily make new practices part of their routine. If you are one of those people, you can immediately incorporate the practices that you feel are most productive for you. Others have not yet developed the discipline to use a new practice, even if they know it is essential for their well-being. If you are in this group, would you consider asking a friend to do an experiment with you? This experiment is a way to support you in remembering to practice what you feel is important. Ask a friend, whom you can think of as a spiritual buddy, to remind you daily of your intention regarding your practices. This is especially helpful with practices that you find yourself resisting.

Go at your own pace. You can select one practice and do it for a day, and then another for the next day, and so on. You can also choose one practice and do that one for a week, or a month, or until you are ready to move on. Utilize the practices in any way that is useful for you. Have your spiritual buddy check in with you every other day. Remember that it is your responsibility to keep your commitment. Your spiritual buddy's commitment is to check in with you, not to take responsibility for you.

Some people will read this book, understand it, and never stop to do the practices, even if they think the practices are good. It will be hard for them to slow down enough to see their great value. Their experiences will be entirely intellectual, and disconnected from their bodies. You cannot become emotionally aware just by thinking about it. Therefore, you will not gain as much from this book if you do not take the time to do the practices, especially if that is difficult for you.

Becoming emotionally aware is a process. Creating authentic power is a lifelong endeavor. The authentic power practices that we have included in this book work for us. When you do them, allow yourself to think about other authentic power practices that might work for you, and create your own. You will discover many. Eventually, your life will become an authentic power practice.

The information in each chapter of this book is part of a whole that is necessary to understanding the heart of emotional awareness. You may think some of the chapters do not apply to you, but, upon reflection, you may be surprised. At the least, they will increase your ability to appreciate other people and their challenges. When you can see the challenges of others with detachment, you are better able to see your own.

Emotional awareness is more than applying techniques to this circumstance or that circumstance. It is a natural expression of an orientation that turns your attention toward the most noble, fulfilling, joyful, and empowering part of yourself that you can reach for. That is your soul.

Cocreation is more than collaboration. Cocreation occurs when individuals bring all that each can offer to a joint effort and, at the same time, open themselves to a larger, or higher, idea that may not have previously occurred to any of them. They do not seek to impose their opinions, but to find a way together to a solution that satisfies all of them completely. They are not content with compromise. They seek the satisfaction of cocreation. They will not cease until each of them says, "Yes. This feels just right to me. This is perfect."

The Heart of the Soul feels that way to both of us. It has been a gift for us to cocreate, and it is a gift for us to share.

With love,
Gary Zukav and Linda Francis

PART I

Fundamentals

The New Species

THE NEED TO FEEL SAFE, valuable, and loved is at the core of human experience. It is a need that is as deep as the need for food and shelter. This need has created hunting, agriculture, and shelter. It has also created clothing, communities, nation-states, and education. It has created science, transportation and communication technologies, furniture, and every object that is not found in nature. It is a need that has propelled us to observe carefully what lies around us and to use it effectively.

Since the origin of the human species, the need to feel safe, valuable, and loved has focused our attention outward toward what is external. It has caused us to study the mineral, plant, and animal kingdoms and to use them in the service of ourselves. Even in cultures in which these kingdoms were honored, such as native cultures, the goal was a harmonious relationship with them that enhanced the probabilities of human survival.

We are so used to reaching outward to satisfy that need that we scarcely notice it. It has become natural, and, for millennia, it has worked. Creating shelters, finding food, raising children, and sending them to school have made countless human beings feel safe, valuable, and loved.

It doesn't work anymore. The same need remains, but looking or reaching outward no longer satisfies it. This is a problem because the habit of looking and reaching outward is still strong, and most people do it without thinking. That is why we are writing this book. The need to feel safe, valuable, and loved can no longer be satisfied merely by surviving, or by engaging in activities that enhance the probability of survival. The feelings that formerly came with sitting around the fire, sharing food from the hunt, and sleeping warmly under fur robes through cold nights are no longer fulfilling in the ways they once were.

Our satisfaction now comes through using our lives, homes, friendships, and communities for a greater goal: spiritual growth. The human species knows how to feed and clothe itself. It knows how to protect itself and to nurture Life. Developing more external power—the ability to manipulate and control those things that appear to be external—will not solve the problems that confront us with increasing severity. **Billions of humans live in poverty, are hungry, and suffer oppression, humiliation, and brutality. Changing these circumstances requires our hearts.** It requires developing the ability

"Changing requires
our hearts."

to feel the pain and joy of others, and to take their needs as seriously as we take our own.

Faster aircraft, space colonies, the internet, and increased agricultural efficiency have no power to make us compassionate and wise. Neither do larger homes or more cars. Compassion and wisdom are the products of spiritual growth. They cannot be centrally planned, mass-produced, or globally distributed. They do not depend upon economies of scale, advertising, and cheap labor. They are not matters of policy but of personal intention. They are the fruits of intense labor, but that labor is inward.

Neither the information age nor the service industry can provide compassion and wisdom. No individual can give compassion or wisdom to another, yet all individuals are now feeling a hunger for them, and that hunger will not quit. The starving mothers and their starving children, the homeless and the unloved, the poor and the sick, the prisoners and their captors, and the billions who live in inner anguish are with us always, because we are beginning to realize that we are inseparable from one another. Their pain is ours, and our pain is theirs. Their joy is ours, and our joy is theirs. Survival to experience needless pain, to give and receive brutality, and to oppress and exploit

"...we are inseparable
from one another."

one another and the Earth is not satisfying, no matter how secure our survival becomes.

**Spiritual growth is now replacing survival as the cen-
tral objective of the human experience.** Spiritual growth is
becoming attractive to individuals from every culture, race, sex,
economic status, and religion. Even while so many humans suffer from brutality, poverty, and starvation, the goal of spiritual
growth is calling us to greater accomplishments than providing
protection, food, and money. It is creating new and deeper understanding of who we are and what our purposes are.

BEYOND SURVIVAL

**Do this simple exercise of looking at your life to see why you
do the things that you do and have the things that you have.
Look deeply. Spend some quiet time. Consider why you eat,
exercise, have the car that you do, have the partner you do,
have the home that you do. Ask yourself, "Do I do this for survival? To feel better about myself? To feel more secure?"**

Spiritual growth—looking inward—is replacing the pursuit
of external power—reaching outward to manipulate and control—as the cure for the insecurity at the core of human experience. Instead of rearranging external circumstances in order to
make ourselves feel more safe, valuable, and loved, **we are
learning how to look inside ourselves to find the roots of
our insecurities and to pull them.**

Getting a new wife or husband, a larger home, or a better
car are all ways of pursuing external power—attempting to

*" ... learning how to look
inside ourselves ... "*

make yourself feel more whole and secure by manipulating and
controlling the external world. So is every use of intelligence,
beauty, wealth, education, muscles, and the latest hair style. Every
attempt to acquire external power now produces only violence
and destruction. The pursuit of external power produces physical violence and destruction between nations. You can see this
in every newscast. The pursuit of external power produces emotional violence and destruction between individuals. You can
verify this yourself. Try persuading a friend to do something
that he or she doesn't want to do, and persist in that effort.

**It is not skill, talent, homes, or cars that produce de-
structive consequences. It is the intention to use them to
manipulate and control others in order to make yourself
feel valuable and loved.** It is not the development of the internet, space colonies, and increased agricultural efficiency that
produce them. It is the intention of the human species to see itself as superior to all else by creating them. So long as we reach
outward in any way to soften the pain of feeling unworthy, or

the terror of not belonging, we bring violence and destruction into our lives, individually and collectively.

TAKE AN INVENTORY

Consider every activity that you do daily. Go through your day, beginning with when you wake, and take an inventory of your actions and your belongings. Ask these questions for everything that you do or have:

"Do I do or have this to survive?"

"Do I do or have this to feel more secure?"

"Do I do or have this to feel better about myself?"

"Do I do or have this to feel better than others?"

"Do I do or have this to be safer?"

For every Yes, ask yourself, "How could I see the things that I do or have differently?" For example, "Instead of eating to make myself feel good, or to feel more secure, I eat so that I can take care of my body." "Instead of having my husband or wife to feel better about myself, or safer, I am with my husband or wife to be in a true partnership."

Make this a habit: Before you do anything, ask yourself, "What is my intention for doing this?"

What enabled our species to survive for so long is now bad medicine. In fact, it is poison. We need homes, agriculture, and technology, but not to make ourselves feel superior to one another and to the rest of Life. We need them to accomplish the goals of the soul, the objectives that bring us together rather than move us apart. We need them to create means of cooperation rather than of competition. We need them to coordinate the activities of sharing rather than of hoarding. We need them to share our perceptions of the sacred.

As long as there are parts of yourself that reach outward to make you feel safe, valuable, and loved, you need to identify them and heal them. These are the parts of yourself that search for security through the cultivation of a particular appearance, new clothes, a larger house, and anything else that makes you feel more at home in the Universe and accepted by your fellow souls.

The Universe is your home, and your fellow souls are each confronting circumstances that are as difficult and challenging for them as yours are for you. They are your colleagues and you are theirs. We are each learning in a special environment in which all that needs to be examined and brought to health in each individual is revealed to her or him in the intimacy of her or his personal experience.

This learning environment is the Earth school. It is a very big school. Everything that the five senses can detect is part of it—from the most distant stars to the most elementary subatomic particles. You, your family, your friends, and everyone else are in the Earth school. In the past, we survived by learning everything that we could about the Earth school. We learned how to find water, grow food, make fire, and build shelters. We developed science and technology. None of these things will now help us to evolve further.

The direction of our attention is shifting one hundred and eighty degrees. We are learning how to turn around and see what we never noticed before—our internal landscape. A new human species is being born. The difference between it and the old species is this: The new species knows that what is behind our eyes is more important than what is in front of them. **The new human species looks at the external world of things, interactions, and experiences as a mirror that reflects an internal world of intentions, emotions, and thoughts.**

EARTH SCHOOL

Close your eyes. Imagine you are in the biggest classroom you have ever seen. There are no walls or doors that can contain it. It includes everything that we can see, hear, taste, smell, and touch. Everything you do here is part of your learning. There is no place that is not rich with learning opportunities.

Learning to see our inner experiences as primary, and our external circumstances as secondary, is the new frontier for the human species. The old species explored the physical world, and it created security by manipulating and controlling what it discovered.

The new species creates security by looking inward to find the causes of insecurity and healing them. This is the path to authentic power.

Authentic Power

AUTHENTIC POWER **is the alignment of your personality with your soul.** Creating authentic power is dramatically different from the pursuit of external power. We know how to pursue external power well because we have been pursuing it since the origin of our species. That is why it is very challenging to discover that it no longer leads us where we want to go. It once produced beneficial consequences, but now it produces only consequences that are counterproductive.

The creation of authentic power is a lifetime endeavor. It requires becoming aware, moment by moment, of what you are feeling and the decisions that you are making. **The creation of authentic power confronts you with the most unhealthy parts of yourself—the parts that blame, criticize, judge, resent, envy, and hate others, yourself, and the Universe.** These are the parts that must be uncovered, acknowledged, and changed. They are also the parts that most want to change others rather than be changed themselves.

This book is part of a course in authentic power. This course provides you with the tools that you need to create authentic power. Whether you use them is up to you. You will not become authentically powerful by simply reading books, attending seminars, or watching television programs. Your life will change only when you decide to change it.

NOTICING UNHEALTHY PARTS

How do you know that you have encountered a part of yourself that wants to change others and the world rather than be changed itself?

Notice when:

You feel right

You feel defensive

You feel angry

You blame others, yourself, or the Universe

You are self-critical

You are upset

You judge others

Anytime you are in a painful reaction
to something or someone

Begin to notice when you feel these things as you go through your day. Each time you notice one of these reactions, congratulate yourself!

Changing your life does not mean getting a new job, husband or wife, or moving away from your parents or back in with them. It means locating within you impulses to make yourself feel worthy by attempting to control others or the circumstances around you, and changing them.

When you become your own source of worthiness, you will still buy clothes, live in a house, and get haircuts. The difference is that you will not do these things to influence or impress others. You will choose your intentions consciously, not unconsciously. You will be free to say and do what is most appropriate, guided by your compassionate heart and your wisdom. You will live without fear. You will give all that you were born to give and receive all that the Universe offers to you. You will live in harmony with others while remaining true to yourself.

WHAT DO YOU WANT TO CHANGE?

Make a list of what you want to change in yourself. For example:

"Power struggles I have with my partner."

"My discomfort with authority figures."

"My resentment that she got the job I wanted."

Authentic power is being fully engaged in the present moment. It is being creative without limitation. It is enjoying the company of all life. It is caring and being cared for. It is being aware of everything that you are feeling, all of the time. It is living in joy. It is being so powerful that the idea of showing power through the use of force is not even a part of your consciousness.

This is the life that now calls you. The values, perceptions, and goals of the new human species do not emerge fully developed. We are all engaged in a process that is taking each of us to

"It is caring and being cared for."

a fuller, richer, more comprehensive perception and understanding of ourselves and the Universe. We are beginning to glimpse a new way of living on the Earth that is more fulfilling and powerful than was possible for the old human species. We are awakening to ourselves as the creators of our experiences, and our responsibility for what we create.

Authentic power is the human experience without the limitations of fear, self-doubt, and self-hatred. When you locate and challenge the parts of yourself that judge, criticize, despair, envy, and hate, you remove the parts of yourself that stand between you and authentic power. When you locate and nurture the parts of yourself that appreciate all of Life, including your own life, you cultivate authentic power.

It is natural to long for harmony, cooperation, sharing, and reverence for Life. These are the intentions of an authentically empowered individual. As you begin to see the differences between your life and a life of harmony, cooperation, sharing, and reverence, you begin the process of creating authentic power. Creating authentic power is reducing those differences to zero.

This book will help you do that. It contains practices that you can use to bring you closer to your soul. These are authentic power practices. Without them, you will not be able to create authentic power. Without authentic power, your life will continue to be painful.

Creating authentic power is a proactive, lifetime endeavor that requires your intention and effort. If you become distracted or get tired, realize that these experiences, also, are part of the creation of authentic power. Authentic power is the experience of fulfillment, no matter what you are doing. It is knowing that the person you are with is the person you are supposed to be with. All that you say and all that you do is appropriate. You have no thoughts of fear.

Many people have brief experiences of authentic power. You may have felt it while you were cooking a meal for a friend or caring for someone who is ill. You may have felt it while getting on a bus to take you somewhere you knew you should be. Linda and I experience it often in our workshops, when we are writing, and when we are aware of each other and the privilege of being together. We experience it often when we are with friends, and when we are alone, each in our own way, with the beauty of Nature.

REMEMBERING

Take some quiet time and remember the times in your life when you had experiences of authentic power. Remember how you felt and what you were thinking. How have these experiences had an impact on your life?

Wishful thinking is not the same as determination. Authentic power cannot be created by wishing for it. It cannot be created by understanding it. You must travel beyond the territory of your mind. Good ideas are one thing. Putting them into practice is another.

The first step in creating authentic power requires you to become aware of everything that you are feeling, all of the time. It is not enough to experience peaks of emotions, such as anger, jealousy, despair, and joy. Your emotions are the force field of your soul. **You cannot align your personality with your soul without becoming conscious of your emotions.**

The Earth school is not an assembly line in which authentically empowered individuals are produced. It is a learning environment in which each individual encounters circumstances tailored for his or her spiritual growth. Recognizing the potential for spiritual growth that each moment presents you, and moving into that potential, is your job.

An authentically empowered person is in partnership with the Universe. The more he or she develops this partnership, the more authentically empowered his or her life becomes. This is the journey of spiritual growth. We are all students in the Earth school and we are all taking the same course: authentic power—what it is, how to create it, and how to use it.

Emotions

EMOTIONS ARE CURRENTS of energy that run through you. They are more than consequences of chemical interactions, hormones, and excesses or deficiencies of neurotransmitters. These are five-sensory explanations of the emotional process. They result from extensive study of neural, chemical, and molecular structures. They do not take into account the soul, nor the purpose of emotions in human evolution.

Think of yourself as a walking processing system. Air flows into you and then flows out of you. While it is in you, you use it and change it before returning it to the atmosphere. Food also flows into you and out of you. It, too, is transformed in the process. Blood flows into your lungs, is changed in your lungs, and then flows out of them again. You process air, food, and blood each moment. They flow through and you are transformed in the process.

You also process energy. All of your systems that process things that the five senses can detect, such as air, food, and blood, reflect another processing system that the five senses cannot detect. That system processes energy. **Energy continually flows into the top of your head, moves downward through your torso, and then returns to where it came from.** This system operates every moment you are alive, just as your respiratory, digestive, and circulatory systems do. Like them, your life depends upon your energy system. Unlike them, you cannot observe your energy system under a microscope, dissect it, or manipulate it pharmaceutically.

All respiratory systems have lungs and muscles to inflate and deflate lungs. Beyond that, each is unique. No lung is exactly like any other. A lung is far too complex to allow for duplication. Each is as distinguishable as its owner. Have you ever seen identical humans? There are none. Identical twins are not identical, even if they look alike. They have different talents, interests, desires, and goals. It is only superficially that they appear to be "identical."

The same is true for all human processing systems. Your digestive system is unique. You have allergies that others do not. You respond to certain foods in ways that others do not. The conditions in your digestive system are different each moment. The process of digestion is similar in all digestive systems, but each is so complex that no two are alike. Food flows easily through some digestive systems, and is transformed effortlessly. These digestive systems function smoothly and efficiently. In other digestive systems food stagnates. These systems are painful and inefficient.

Your energy system is unique, too. Some energy systems function smoothly and effortlessly, and others are turbulent and tiring. Each is unique, even though all of them have fundamental similarities.

Energy enters your body at the top of your head and is processed at different locations in your energy system as it moves downward through your torso, just as food enters your body through your mouth and is processed at different places in your digestive system. Food goes into your stomach, then your upper intestine, and then your lower intestine. At each location, different processes occur.

A similar thing happens in your energy system. **As energy is processed at different locations, and in different ways, different emotions result.** When energy is processed in one way at one location, one kind of emotion, such as anger, is produced. When it is processed in another way at the same location, another type of emotion is produced, such as delight. Your emotions tell you how energy is being processed, and at which locations.

Once you understand your emotions in this way, you can use them to see how your energy system is functioning. You can look at your emotions, such as guilt, sadness, fear, and anger as the result of the different ways that energy is being processed in your energy system.

You can change your experience of food as it moves through your digestive system by taking something alkaline, such as baking soda, if you have too much acid in your stomach. Or, if the energy from the food that you are eating is not absorbed efficiently into your body, you can take enzymes. However, baking soda will not help your intestines absorb energy from your food, and enzymes will not reduce the amount of acid in your stomach. You have to know what to take in each case in order to change your experience and to do that, you have to understand your digestive system.

The same is true of your energy system. You can change the experiences that are generated by the energy moving through your energy system, but in order to do that you have to understand how the system works. Those experiences are your emotions.

You can change the experiences that are caused by food moving through your digestive system by eating different foods. The energy that flows into it is always pure and wholesome. It remains that way as it moves through your energy system, is transformed, and then returned to where it came from. You cannot change the nature of this energy, but you can change how you experience it by changing the way that it is processed.

WHOLESOME ENERGY

Say to yourself, "The energy that flows into me is always pure and wholesome."

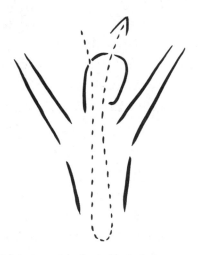

*"The energy that flows into me
is always pure and wholesome."*

You cannot grow spiritually without learning how to detach from your emotions and understand them as products of the way energy is processed in your energy system. If you become angry, for example, and you cannot detach from your anger, you will shout, withdraw emotionally, or enact one of the many other ways that angry people express themselves. When you become happy and you cannot detach from your happiness, you become uncontrollably elated, buoyant, or exhilarated.

RECOGNIZING EMOTIONS

Feel your body in the area of your head, then your neck, chest, abdomen, and pelvis. Notice if there is any tightness, pain, or other sensations.

The next time you feel angry, hurt, upset, or jealous, notice these same areas in your body, and see how they feel then.

Your emotions—whether anger or happiness or any others—do not depend upon what is happening outside of you but upon how your energy system is processing energy. Changing another individual or circumstance may alter your emotions temporarily, but your energy system will always generate another emotion. If you believe that this new emotion depends upon people or circumstances, you will have to change something or someone else again.

Recognizing that your emotions come from your energy system, and not from your interactions with people or things, is important. You cannot always change people or circumstances, but you can always change the way energy is processed in your energy system. You only have to know where and how energy is being processed, and that is what your emotions tell you.

---

*Your emotions
come from your
ENERGY SYSTEM,
not your
interactions
with
people
or
things.*

Each emotion is a message for you, a signal from your soul. If you do not pay attention to the signal, another will come. The message is important, and your soul will not let you forget about it. When you look at your emotions as obstacles, or experiences that you would rather have or not have, you miss the point. The point is that every emotion offers information about you that is important. When you ignore your emotions, you ignore this information.

Friends support friends through difficulties. The best of friends is the one who stays through the most difficult times. **Your emotions are the best of friends. They do not leave you. They continually bring to your attention what you need to know.** The more important that information is to you, the more forcefully they call to you.

EVERY EMOTION IS A MESSAGE

Think of a time when you felt a strong emotion, such as anger, happiness, jealousy, or resentment.

Close your eyes and go back to that time. Take a few minutes to feel what this emotion felt like in your body. Where did you feel it? (For example, in your chest, stomach, pelvis, neck, throat?)

Remember what thoughts you were having when you experienced this emotion. (For example, if you were angry, were you blaming yourself, someone else, or a situation?)

Remember what you said when you experienced this emotion. (For example, if you were resentful, did you say something hurtful?)

Remember how you behaved. (For example, if you were happy, did you laugh or dance?)

If you knew that your emotion was a message from your soul, would you have changed what you did or said while you experienced this emotion?

What would you have done differently?

Once you trust a friend, you look forward to his every visit. You accept her gifts with gratitude. You savor them and hold them dear. Your emotions bring you the most precious gift that the Universe can give. They tell you how your energy system is processing energy. Without that knowledge you cannot change. With it, you know exactly what needs to be changed and how.

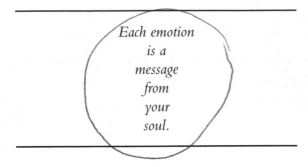

Each emotion is a message from your soul.

No counselor can give you that information. No teacher, parent, or priest can, either. Your emotions are a song written only for you.

Your job is to listen.

The Earth School

IMAGINE A BOY WHO SELLS NEWSPAPERS on a city corner, holding the latest edition above his head and shouting the headline. That is what happens when you experience an emotion. The more important the headline is, the stronger the emotion is. Keeping current with the news is something that you have to decide to do, but the newspaper boy is always shouting the latest headline.

The next day, he will be waiting for you with another headline. When you turn on your television, it will show you the same headline. You can turn off the television and cancel your subscription to the newspaper, but you cannot turn off or cancel your emotions. **Even if you are not aware of your emotions, they are always being produced inside you.** The energy that flows through your energy system never stops, and your energy system never stops functioning.

Each emotion has different characteristics. Anger disappears more quickly than jealousy. The need for revenge is more persistent than jealousy. Some emotions come more frequently than others, and some stay longer than others. This flow of emotions is like a shower. The shower of your emotions continues until you leave the Earth school—until you die. It is a flow that never stops, whether you pay attention to it or not. You may daydream for a while, but sooner or later you wake up in the shower.

Your emotions always return, too. Each time they show you where and how energy is being processed in your energy system. When you understand that system, you will know why you are experiencing an emotion and how you can change it, if you want to change it.

Your emotional landscape is unique, just as your body, aptitudes, and interests are unique. It is like your fingerprint, except that it is more familiar because you experience it continually. It is so familiar that you might think that everyone's emotional landscape is like yours. That is not correct.

You may become angry easily, another person may become frightened, and yet another may become jealous. You may shout when you are angry. Some people withdraw and become silent. Some people are frightened to be alone. They need to be in the company of others to feel safe. Some people are frightened when they are with others. They need to be alone to feel safe. Some people need to talk. They become frightened when they are silent. Others need to listen. They become frightened when they speak.

As you become aware of your emotions, you also become aware of your curriculum in the Earth school. In other words, the emotions in your emotional landscape are your particular course of study in the Earth school. **Everyone in the Earth school takes the same course—authentic power—but different students need to take different classes in order to complete it.**

Every painful emotion is a class. If you are angry, you are in that class. If you are jealous, you are in that class. If you are angry and jealous, you are in both classes. Not every class on anger is the same, and not every class on jealousy is the same. Becoming emotionally withdrawn when you are angry is one class. Becoming bossy and loud when you are angry is another. Every healthy emotion, such as appreciation, gratitude, contentment, and joy, is also a class. There are different ways of experiencing each of these emotions, too, and each of them is yet another class.

The Earth school has more classes than can be printed in a catalog. You do not need to take all of them. You are automatically enrolled in certain classes when you enter the Earth school—when you are born. You graduate from a class when you understand what you need to know about that particular emotion. When you complete your assigned classes, you are given the opportunity to choose other classes. For example, you are allowed to enroll in the joy class after you have completed the anger and jealousy classes. You may have glimpses of the joy class before you graduate from the anger and jealousy classes, but you will not be able to study joy full-time until you do. You are allowed to enroll in the gratitude class after you have completed the sadness class, and so on.

There are two types of classes in the Earth school— classes about fear and classes about love. Anger, vengefulness, sadness, and greed are classes about fear. Joy and gratitude are classes about love. When you begin to see your emotions in this way, all of the circumstances that you encounter in your life will become meaningful to you. You begin to look at them all as circumstances that are perfect for bringing your attention to inner dynamics that you need to examine and change. These are your painful emotions.

LIST YOUR CLASSES

Take some time to look inside yourself and see what classes you are enrolled in (for example, anger, sorrow, jealousy, rage, fear, vengefulness, resentfulness, appreciation, gratitude, contentment, joy, etc.).

Make a list. Notice whether these classes are about fear or about love. If you are brave enough, do this with a friend.

Your emotions become the focus of your attention, not the people or circumstances that appear to be causing your emotions. Instead of being angry at an individual or circumstance—or depressed, jealous, or frightened—be grateful that they have brought particular emotions to your attention. **Instead of trying to change circumstances or people, examine the emotions you are experiencing.**

These emotions come from inside you, not from outside. They come as old friends. You may think that your anger is justified, but if you look at your anger instead of the injustice that you think causes it, you will see that your anger is very familiar. You have felt the same way at other times and in other places with other people in other circumstances. The times, places, people, and circumstances change, but your anger does not. Nor does your sadness, vengefulness, or fear.

When you make this connection you are in a position to change your life. You cannot change all of the people that make you angry, jealous, or sad, but you can change yourself. When you know how to do that, how other people speak or act is not as important to you as how you respond to them. Trying to change others when you are angry is the same as trying to

The Guest House

This being human is a guest house.
Every morning a new arrival.

A joy, a depression, a meanness,
some momentary awareness comes
as an unexpected visitor.

Welcome and entertain them all!
Even if they're a crowd of sorrows,
who violently sweep your house
Empty of its furniture,
Still, treat each guest honorably.
He may be clearing you out
for some new delight.

The dark thought, the shame, the malice,
meet them at the door laughing,
and invite them in.

Be grateful for whoever comes,
because each has been sent
as a guide from beyond.

—Rumi

The Essential Rumi, Coleman Barks, trans. (New York: HarperCollins, 1995), p. 109.

change your reflection in a mirror. You can rage at your reflection as long as you wish, but until you change what is being reflected, your rage will not leave.

Looking inward instead of focusing on outward circumstances is an important step in the process of spiritual development. When you take it you begin the process of shifting your goal from the pursuit of external power—the ability to manipulate and control—to the pursuit of authentic power—the alignment of your personality with your soul.

Imagine yourself as a student. You are in a school that is always in session. You have a special tutor who ensures that you are taught exactly what you need to learn. The tutor takes into account what you already know and what you have accomplished previously. Your tutor is patient, wise, and compassionate. You choose how quickly or slowly you will learn. Your tutor works intimately with you, and utilizes every one of your decisions to provide experiences that offer you the greatest potential to move forward in your education.

BE A STUDENT

Every morning when you wake up, remind yourself that you are a student in the Earth school, and that everything that happens this day is to help you learn.

Every night go over all the things that happened in school. Did you remember that you were in school? How often did you remember? What classes did you attend today? (Anger, joy, jealousy, sorrow, etc.)

The Universe is your tutor. **Your classroom is your life.** Everything that happens within it is part of your custom-crafted curriculum. You cannot fail this school. Sooner or later you will graduate from it. You can ignore your assignments, and take the same classes as many times as you choose. You can also apply yourself and accelerate your process.

By becoming aware of your emotions, you wake up as a student in the Earth school. You have been a student in the Earth school since you were born. Your emotions show you what to work on next. **Your task as a student in the Earth school is**

not to change your parents, boss, employees, or classmates. It is to change yourself.

Your most painful emotions show you what you are most resistant to changing. They are the ones that occur most often because you have failed to do your homework, and your progress in the Earth school has halted at that class. You find yourself in other classes, but more and more of those classes are related to the class that you refuse to take seriously. Some people even think that the class that they will not seriously study, such as their depression, rage, jealousy, or vengefulness, is ruining their lives. Actually, that class especially contains exactly what they need to remedy a type of illness that has grown both chronic and acute—that has lasted a very long time and has become very painful.

Studying a subject seriously does not mean reading about it, discussing it, and writing papers. It means looking inside yourself. That begins when you experiment with the idea that you, and not other people, are the cause of your emotions. When you hold that idea, you stop trying to explain how people and circumstances make you feel the way you feel.

Studying a class seriously
is more than
reading, understanding, discussing, and writing.
If you want to pass this class
you need to
look inside yourself.
Assume that you are the cause of emotions that torment you,
not
other people or things.

If you break a bone in your foot, your foot will not stop hurting until you tend to it. The pain is not the problem. The pain is calling your attention to a problem. Painful emotions do the same thing. They call your attention to what needs to be healed in you in order for you to reach your fullest potential.

You cannot heal a broken bone by blaming the ladder that fell while you were on it. You also cannot stop a painful emotion by shouting at people or things, or withholding your love. They are not the cause of your painful emotions. The cause of your painful emotions is the way energy is being processed in your energy system.

You cannot heal the cause of your painful emotions
by
shouting, getting even, withdrawing
or
any way that takes your focus from your feelings
because
the cause is the way that energy is processed in your
energy system.

Directing your attention toward your energy system and away from external circumstances allows you to begin the process of making permanent changes in yourself.

Only you can make permanent changes in yourself.

Processing Energy, Part 1

YOUR ENERGY SYSTEM HAS SEVEN CENTERS. **As energy flows through each center in your energy system, it creates different experiences in you. Those experiences are your emotions.**

In order to understand your emotions, it is necessary to understand these different energy centers, where they are, and what they do. Your energy system is not detectable by X ray or

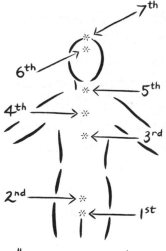

"Your energy system has seven centers."

magnetic resonance imaging. Its centers cannot be found in particular organs or cells, but they are as real as your organs and cells. They cannot be seen, heard, touched, smelled, or tasted. They are undetectable by the five senses but they are not undetectable by your inner experiences. They *are* your inner experiences.

The seventh center is at the crown of your head.

This is where energy enters your energy system. This center connects you with the nonphysical Universe. That connection remains active as long as you live. When you go home—return to nonphysical reality—your energy system ceases to function, and your personality dies.

Your personality is your body, your intuitional structure (how you experience intuition), and the particular ways that you perceive, think, and feel. Your personality was born on a certain date, and it will die on a certain date. That is the date that your energy system stops functioning. It is also the date that your other systems, such as digestive, respiratory, and circulatory, stop functioning. As long as you live, energy flows into your energy system through the center at the crown of your head and moves downward to the base of your torso. Then it reverses direction, moves upward, and leaves your energy system where it entered. It also leaves your energy system through the other six centers at the same time.

There are two ways energy can leave your energy system: in fear and doubt or in love and trust. Throughout your life you choose, from moment to moment, whether you will learn through fear and doubt or through love and trust. No matter which way you choose, energy continues to enter your energy system at the crown of your head and leave through each of the centers in your energy system.

When energy leaves a center in fear and doubt, it produces an experience. When it leaves that center in love and trust, it produces a different experience. Each of the centers in your energy system produces a different experience, depending upon whether it radiates energy in fear and doubt or in love and trust. **No matter where or how energy leaves your energy system, it produces an emotion.**

Fear and doubt produce painful emotions, such as anger, jealousy, grief, and vengefulness. When energy leaves a center in fear and doubt, the result is always painful. Love and trust produce positive emotions, such as gratitude, contentment, and joy. Positive emotions are always produced when energy leaves a center in love and trust.

An authentically powerful individual is one who has learned to release his or her energy in love and trust. To become authentically empowered, you must learn the difference between releasing your energy in love and trust and releasing it in fear and doubt.

Your emotions tell you how and where energy leaves your energy system. They provide you with information. Painful emotions are not obstacles to a happy life. They are road signs that show you the direction that you must travel if you want to create a happy life. That direction is always toward your emotions.

Every painful emotion tells you that you are releasing energy in fear and doubt.

There is no other way to create a painful emotion. When you become familiar with your emotions and your energy system, you will be able to see how each of your centers is radiating energy and whether energy is leaving them in love and trust or in fear and doubt. This is emotional awareness.

Any painful emotion means you are
Acting
Speaking
Thinking
in
Fear and doubt.

You may think that your anger comes from an interaction with a rude person, but it does not. It comes from energy leaving your energy system in fear and doubt. You may think that your sorrow comes from the death of a friend, but it does not. It comes from energy leaving your energy system in fear and doubt. The cause of your emotions may appear to be lack of money, losing a relationship, getting what you want, or getting what you do not want. Beneath these appearances lie fundamental issues pertaining to the way you process energy. Until you shift your attention away from appearances and onto these issues, you will continue to experience painful emotions.

The sixth center is in your forehead, between your eyes.

This center allows you to see more than your five senses can show you. It allows you to know the intentions of others, even if they do not express them. It enables you to recognize the opportunities that your experiences offer you to grow spiritually. It shifts your orientation from that of victim of your experiences to that of creator of your experiences. This center provides bearings for you on the ocean of your experiences. It allows you to see how the Earth school works, and the perfection of it.

A new human species is being born as this center becomes active in individual after individual. It is becoming active within you, or you would not be reading this book. When this center becomes active, you see the entire physical universe—stars and galaxies, mountains and clouds, and rocks and oceans—as part of a greater nonphysical Universe. Nothing appears random.

When energy leaves this center in love and trust, you see the wisdom and compassion of the Universe wherever you look. When it leaves in fear and doubt, what you see appears cold and frightening. In the first case, a path through the woods appears sunlit and welcoming. In the second case, the same path appears dark and foreboding. When you see the path one way, it invites you forward. When you see it the second way, it frightens you. When this center processes energy in love and trust, you become clear. You see the purpose of everything in your life, including your emotions.

Processing Energy, Part 2

EVERY EMOTION IS A PHYSICAL EXPERIENCE. Emotions are physical sensations that occur in different parts of your body. When energy leaves through a center in your energy system, it produces physical sensations.

Emotional awareness is noticing what sensations you are feeling in your body, and where. These sensations and their locations are important. They show how you are processing the energy flowing through your energy system.

The painful sensations that are produced when energy leaves one center in fear and doubt are different from the painful sensations that are produced when energy leaves another center in fear and doubt. You can feel the difference. The positive physical sensations produced when energy leaves one center in love and trust are different from the positive sensations produced when it leaves other centers in love and trust. You can feel those differences, too.

Your energy system continually produces physical sensations in the vicinity of each of its centers. Those sensations are your emotions. Your emotions tell you how each center is radiating energy—in love and trust or in fear and doubt.

When the energy that is flowing downward through the

centers in your energy system reaches the fifth center, it is easy
to feel the sensations that it produces. This center is in the vicinity of your throat.

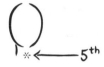

When energy leaves the fifth center in love and trust, you
express yourself clearly and easily. Your voice is full and strong. It
does not waver, it is not tentative. When energy leaves this center in fear and doubt, your expression is constricted and you
cannot convey what you feel. Your throat or neck becomes
tight. Speaking is like forcing water through a hose that has been
pinched. The dribble that makes it through the constriction is
small compared with the force of the water dammed up behind
it. Your voice is weak and hoarse. You cough or clear your
throat frequently.

These symptoms—a clear, strong voice or a weak, fragile
voice; a relaxed throat or a tight, constricted throat; a free flow
of words or urges to cough or clear your throat—tell you
whether energy is leaving this center in love and trust or in fear
and doubt. **The departure of energy from your energy
system is a real event that produces physical experiences, which can be observed easily when you focus
your attention on your body.** These physical experiences tell
you not only where—through which center—you are radiating
energy, they also tell you how you are radiating it.

**Recognizing where and how energy leaves your en-
ergy system is the foundation of spiritual growth.** You

cannot be authentically empowered and ignore your fears at the same time. Ignoring your emotions is ignoring your fears as well as your joy. **All of your emotions originate in the same place—your energy system.** Every emotion calls your attention to this system. Sooner or later you will come to terms with it. When you do, you begin the spiritual journey.

FREE SPEECH

Imagine talking to a friend you feel safe with. Notice how you feel in the area of your throat and neck. Notice the quality of your voice. Do you feel any obstruction in your throat? Do you feel you are expressing yourself clearly?

Imagine talking to someone who is intimidating. How do your throat and neck feel now? What is the quality of your voice? Do you feel any obstruction in your throat? Do you feel that you are expressing what you want to express?

Now practice doing these exercises the next time you are in a real conversation. Notice whether your throat and neck feel relaxed or tense, whether your voice is clear and strong or weak and raspy, and whether you are really saying what you want to express.

The first three centers form a group. Through this group energy enters your energy system, enables you to see beyond the limitation of your five senses, and empowers you to express yourself. That is the beginning of its journey.

The next center is in your chest. When energy leaves this center in love and trust, you radiate warmth and compassion. You feel connected to all of Life. Everyone becomes your relative. Plants, animals, birds, and insects also become your relatives. You feel the pain of others and the joy of others. You care for others. You are open and welcoming.

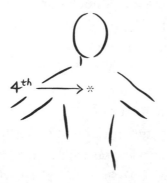

When energy leaves this center in fear and doubt, you are cold and distant. People appear as objects. You are interested in things, not neighbors. Your relationships are superficial; you analyze, compare, and evaluate people the same way that you analyze, compare, and evaluate thoughts and theories. You value those that are useful to you, and dismiss those that are not. You are closed and defensive.

Physical sensations accompany these experiences. When energy leaves this center in fear and doubt, your chest hurts. The pain can be so intense that it feels like a heart attack. Sometimes it is a heart attack. Your shoulders and back are tight. If you do not pay attention to your body, you develop upper-back pain.

"Heartache" is more than an emotional state. It is a physical condition. If you focus on your thoughts of grief for what you have lost, despair for what you cannot accomplish, or resentment toward others, you will not see the source of your pain. You will not be able to change it, either. You will find another of what you have lost, accomplish something else, and get revenge. Your energy system will remain a mystery to you, and it will continue to produce heartaches when energy leaves this center in fear and doubt.

The permanent remedy is not to alter your circumstances. It is to change the way you process energy. That means recognizing when energy leaves this center in fear and doubt, and learning to release it in love and trust. **Before you can change the way you process energy, you must become aware of how you are processing it.** That is what your emotions tell you.

The release of energy in fear and doubt through this center causes pain. You fear that you cannot live without what you have lost. You doubt that you can replace what you have lost. You fear that you cannot become whole again. You doubt that the Universe cares for you. You doubt that you are worth caring for. When large amounts of energy leave through this center in fear and doubt, heartache is intense.

OPEN YOUR HEART

Practice opening your heart by thinking of a time when you felt love and openness for someone—your child, grandchild, partner, friend, or even a stranger. Remember the situation and what you were feeling in the area of your heart.

When you feel your heart is closed (your chest hurts), let yourself experience the pain in your chest, breathe deeply, and, at the same time, remember that special time when you felt open and loving. Go back to it in your imagination. Keep thinking about it and breathing deeply, until you feel yourself begin to relax, even if only a little.

When energy leaves this center in love and trust, you are available to others. You are interested in others. Your chest is relaxed. Your shoulders and back are comfortable. You are open and expansive.

These physical sensations are easy to recognize, but you have to make the effort to look for them. Your energy system is especially effective in alerting you to the release of energy in fear and doubt. When that happens, your body hurts. **Emotional pain of any kind is a reminder to stop and look inside.** When you do, you will discover that your body hurts in specific places. Those places tell you which center is releasing energy in fear and doubt.

The center in your chest is the heart of your energy system. It is at the center. It connects the centers above it with the centers below it. When you see through your heart, feel though your heart, and perceive with your heart, you go directly to the core of the matter. You combine your ability to see clearly and express yourself with your daily activities. You are integrated and integrating. When you learn to release your energy through this center in love and trust, you are open to others and the Universe, grateful for others and the Universe, and strong of heart.

Processing Energy, Part 3

THE NEXT CENTER also produces clearly recognizable physical sensations when it releases energy, and especially when it radiates energy in fear and doubt. This center is near your solar plexus. Your solar plexus is above your stomach and just below your ribs where they come together in the center of your chest. This is the center that you feel when you worry.

When energy leaves this center in fear and doubt, you feel it in the "pit of your stomach." Every organ in the central area of your body is affected when energy leaves this center in fear and doubt, but your stomach is especially sensitive. You feel pain in this area each time you fear that you are not able to accomplish something that is important to you.

In its mildest form, this pain is queasiness, or "butterflies" in the stomach. If you worry long enough about paying your rent, supporting your family, getting the right job, being liked, or anything else, the agitation in your stomach becomes severe. That is when stomach ulcers occur. From the perspective of the five senses—what can be heard, smelled, tasted, and touched—stomach ulcers are the consequence of excessive stomach acid, which is caused by chemical imbalances in the body, which are caused by neuronal firing in the brain, which are caused by neurotransmitters, and so on.

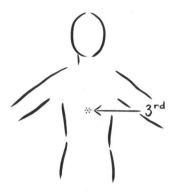

Balancing your body chemistry and reducing acid in your stomach will not reach the root of the problem. The root of the problem is energy leaving this center in fear and doubt. The first step in healing a stomach ulcer is to develop emotional awareness. Developing emotional awareness begins the process of pulling the problem out by the root.

WHAT, ME WORRY?

Get in touch with the physical sensations in your body when you are worrying, for example, about the rent, what to fix for dinner, if your friend is upset with you, if the workman did the job right without you. Feel the physical sensations in your body, especially in the area of your solar plexus (third center).

When energy leaves this center in love and trust, you have no doubt that you can accomplish what you need to accomplish. You do not fear failure. You know that you are the right person in the right place at the right time. Every challenge stimulates you. You are comfortable with your abilities, and grateful for them.

When energy leaves the center at your solar plexus in love

and trust, you are relaxed and confident, open and capable. You feel competent, and you are.

The next energy center is in the region of your reproductive organs. Most people associate this center with sex. It is more than that. It is the seat of your creativity. From it spring new thoughts, insights, perceptions, and understanding. **Each decision is a moment of creativity.** What you create is for you to decide.

When energy leaves this center in fear and doubt, you create ways of exploiting circumstances and others. The release of energy in fear and doubt from this center produces strong sexual cravings. You look for someone to satisfy them. You are not concerned with the well-being of the other individual. You are concerned with your needs. Strangers become magnetically attractive. You fantasize sexual interactions. One individual is as useful to you as the next. All are replaceable.

This type of sexual attraction does not signal the arrival of a "soul mate." It signals the release of energy in fear and doubt from your energy system through the center. The signal is unmistakable. It intrudes upon your consciousness with urgency.

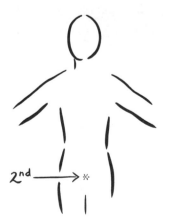

Sexual interaction is a temporary solution. The craving always returns.

The issue is not sexual craving, but energy leaving this center in your energy system in fear and doubt. Until that issue is addressed, the torment of sexual desire will remain. Relationships of substance and depth are not formed quickly or easily. They require effort, patience, courage, love, and trust. They require self-exploration. They illuminate fears and reveal hidden, painful, and shameful parts of yourself. Within this type of relationship, sexual interactions express care and love.

When energy leaves this center in fear and doubt, it transforms you and others into mutual predators, stalking one another. When it leaves in love and trust, it transforms your experiences into cocreative celebrations of Life.

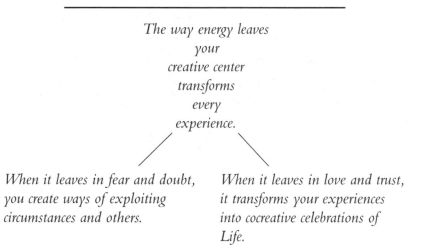

The way energy leaves your creative center transforms every experience.

When it leaves in fear and doubt, you create ways of exploiting circumstances and others.

When it leaves in love and trust, it transforms your experiences into cocreative celebrations of Life.

By recognizing sexual attractions, fantasies, and cravings as information about your energy system and how and where it is processing energy, you begin to gain mastery over some of your most powerful impulses. You begin to examine the dynamics that generate your emotions.

The last energy center is located at the base of your torso, near your genital area. It is at the very bottom of your physical trunk. This center connects you with the Earth.

From the five-sensory perspective, the earth is various strata of rocks and a core of molten lava. From the multisensory perspective that is now emerging throughout the human species, the Earth is a living being of enormous wisdom and compassion. It is the "Mother Earth" of children's tales and Native wisdom. This center is the connection between your energy system and the energy of the living Earth.

This center connects you to the Earth in the same way that the center at the top of your torso connects you to the non-physical Universe. Just as a tree reaches for the sky and the Earth at the same time, your energy system is anchored in the non-physical Universe and in the energy of the Earth at the same time. When energy leaves this center in love and trust, you feel at home on the Earth. The Earth nourishes you, just as a tree is fed by the Earth. You are "grounded."

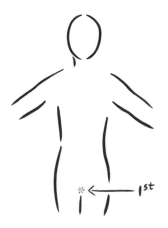

When energy leaves this center in fear and doubt, the Earth does not feel like home. Everything on it becomes a threat. You fear more than the dark of night and falling rocks. You fear your life because you feel you do not belong on the Earth. When you experience stress, you long to leave the Earth. You feel that the sky is your home, and you want to return to it. You think that you are on the Earth by accident. Releasing energy from this center in fear and doubt prevents you from learning what you need to learn while you are on the Earth.

EARTH CONNECTION

Every day take a few minutes to appreciate the Earth. Stand, sit, or lie on the Earth, the grass, the ground, or the floor. Allow yourself to be held, to be nurtured, by the Earth. Even if you are lying on a carpet on a floor, you are being held by the Earth. The floor and carpet are holding you, but what is holding them? Spend at least five minutes. Entrust yourself completely to the Earth for a few minutes each day.

This is sacred time.

Discomfort with your life on the Earth does not prevent you from enjoying a waterfall, a mountain, or a forest, but it prevents you from relaxing into your life. You feel vulnerable, no matter where you are. Beneath this discomfort is a terror of being alive. This terror is painful.

When energy leaves this center in love and trust, you do not fear your life. You are rooted in your experiences, and they nourish you. You grow like a tree, reaching for the sky while anchored on the Earth. You see the rhythm of the Earth—spring to summer to autumn to winter—in your life. You are at home.

By recognizing your desires to be elsewhere and longing to "go home" as emotions that are produced when energy is released from this particular center in fear and doubt, you are no longer at their mercy. The Earth is your home while you are on it. Releasing energy through this center in fear and doubt prevents you from enjoying it. Releasing it in love and trust nourishes, energizes, and heals you.

MAKING FRIENDS WITH YOUR EMOTIONS

Imagine seeing each of your emotions as a present—your anger, joy, sadness, resentment. Each one is a surprise. Say to yourself, "I wonder what I am going to learn about myself from this present."

Without understanding your energy system and how it works, your emotions come as surprises. Sometimes they are pleasant. Sometimes they are painful. With understanding, your emotions become friends—even those that are difficult to experience. They tell you how and where you are processing energy.

Think of your emotions as presents, waiting to be unwrapped.

Unwrapping them is part of the spiritual journey.

"... your emotions as presents..."

Adding Color

ENERGY IS ALWAYS LEAVING each of the centers in your energy system. As it does, it creates an experience that we call an emotion. For example, when you think angry thoughts, you may feel tightness in your chest (fourth center) and butterflies in your stomach (third center) created by energy leaving your energy system through these centers in fear and doubt. As you fantasize a sexual interaction, you feel attracted to someone (second center) and maybe queasiness in your stomach (third center). As you enjoy wildflowers in a meadow, you breathe deeply and feel pleasant sensations in your chest (fourth center), and so on.

PRACTICING THE SCAN

Scan your body. Allow yourself to experience what sensations you are feeling near each energy center, beginning at the crown of your head and moving downward to the base of your torso. If you do not feel anything in one center, go to the next. Then start over. Do this several times until you begin to experience sensations, particularly in your neck, chest, and stomach areas.

Are these sensations pleasant or uncomfortable?

Imagine that you could see each emotion—each physical sensation near a particular energy center—as a different color. **Energy leaving a particular center in fear and doubt (and causing a particular painful sensation) would "light up" that center in a particular way.** Energy is always leaving each of the centers in your energy system, and "lighting up" each one in a particular way as it does. **When energy leaves through every center in love and trust, your energy system is beautiful and radiant.** When energy leaves through every center in your energy system in fear and doubt, your energy system is less pleasing to see, and much less pleasing to experience.

Sometimes energy leaves one center in fear and doubt and another center in love and trust at the same time. For example, you are frightened about a performance review at work and, at the same time, grateful for your friends. You feel butterflies in your stomach (third energy center) while your chest and upper back (fourth center) are relaxed.

When you are aware of the butterflies in your stomach and the relaxed feeling in your chest, you are aware of your emotions. **Feeling your emotions is a physical experience.** Your emotions are physical experiences that you can teach yourself to recognize. Once you recognize them, you will be surprised to discover how many different emotions—physical sensations in your body—you experience at each moment.

Spiritual growth requires you to become aware of everything that you are feeling all of the time. When you were young, you learned to recognize colors by labeling them. Your mother or father would say "green" and point to a color. After a while, you recognized that color. When you did, you repeated the word, "green." You learn to recognize emotions the same way, except that you must make the effort to feel them and label them. A friend might help by saying, "That is nothing to be frightened about," when you did not realize that you were frightened, or "Why are you angry?" when you did not recognize your anger. Even so, it is your job to become aware of your emotions, and identify them.

When you can do this, they will no longer toss you about. You will recognize inner physical sensations to match the labels "joy," "anger," "fear," and "jealousy." Eventually you will become as familiar with your emotions—these sensations—as you are with your best friends. You will recognize them without thinking about their names, just as you can recognize colors without thinking about what they are called.

If you could see your energy system, and the energy that radiates from its centers, you would see some colors more frequently than others. Each time energy leaves a center in fear and doubt, that center "lights up" with the same color. When energy leaves that center in love and trust, it lights up with another color. Some centers light up more often in fear and doubt or in love and trust. They are more often one color than another. One of them may always release energy in fear and doubt, and it remains the same color.

The chronic release of energy in fear and doubt from any center in your energy system produces physical symptoms in the vicinity of that center. Those symptoms may be back pain, sore throat, heart pain, lung congestion, indigestion, headache, urinary infection, and on and on. There are numerous symptoms created by the release of energy in fear and doubt from different centers in your energy system. All of them are painful. There are also numerous symptoms created by the release of energy from different centers in love and trust. All of them feel good.

Noticing the center that is nearest a physical dysfunction when it occurs tells you where your energy system has been losing energy in fear and doubt for a long time, and is continuing to lose energy in fear and doubt. This is valuable information. From a five-sensory perspective, pneumonia is caused by bacteria, heart pain is caused by arterial obstruction, and so on. From that perspective, the prescription for pneumonia is an antibiotic, and heart disease is cured by opening arteries. **The deeper cause of every physical dysfunction is energy leaving your energy system in fear and doubt.**

Drugs cannot alter the way energy leaves your energy system. Neither can surgery. Only you can change that. Changing the way energy leaves your energy system begins with becoming aware of what you are feeling all of the time, and not only when you are intensely angry, sad, jealous, or distressed. **Emotional awareness is preventive medicine.** It allows you to detect circumstances in your energy system that will produce painful dysfunctions in your body long before they appear.

If you do not become aware of those circumstances, you will eventually become aware of the consequences, in the form of illness and pain in your body. **Medical treatment of a physical dysfunction is emergency treatment of a symptom that has developed over a long time.** The symptom is the flower on a plant. It is the last part of the plant to develop. Treating the symptom is picking the flower. The plant remains untouched.

The cause of physical dysfunction, wherever it appears, is the release of energy from your energy system

in fear and doubt for an extended time. A physical symptom cannot appear in your body without the chronic release of energy in fear and doubt from your energy system, any more than a flower can appear without a plant. Medical science is the study of flowers. Spiritual growth is the study of plants. It begins with emotional awareness.

Releasing energy from your energy system in love and trust produces health and vitality. It "lights up" your centers differently. It produces gratitude, joy, and fulfillment. You cannot see these colors, but you can feel them. Your experience fills with love and meaning. You are fully engaged in the present moment. You are buoyant and radiant. You appreciate every circumstance and event, including those that others consider tragic.

This is the experience of energy leaving your energy system in love and trust.

It is also the experience of authentic power.

The Scan

THE INSTRUMENTS IN YOUR CAR give you a continuous reading on the operation of the engine. They tell you if your engine is overheating, charging itself properly, has enough oil pressure and fuel, and is running within its limits. These instruments work whether you look at them or not. The engine runs whether you look at the instruments or not, until the engine malfunctions. Then the instruments show what the malfunction is, but if you are not looking at the instruments, you will not see what they are showing.

An engine can run a little while without charging itself, but sooner or later, it will stop running and cannot be restarted without a charge. Its battery has died. The charge meter on the instrument panel showed when the charging system began to fail. The engine didn't stop running until the charge in the battery was completely gone. The same thing is true of the fuel gauge. When the car is out of gas, it stops running, no matter how finely tuned the engine is. The fuel gauge showed when the fuel became low, but if no one looked at it, no one knew what was happening.

An engine cannot run more than a few moments without oil pressure, or when it is overheating. If these conditions are not changed immediately, the engine is ruined. An engine replacement, which is extremely expensive, is the only alternative. If you do not have access to someone who can replace your engine, you walk, wait, or make other arrangements.

There is no one to replace an engine on an empty road in the night. There is no garage in the forest or in a desert. If the temperature outside is frigid, the inside of the car will become frigid, also, when the engine stops running. Power brakes and power steering do not work when the engine is not running. If the engine stops running when the car is speeding, the situation is extremely dangerous.

All of these circumstances—which range from inconvenient to fatal—can be avoided by looking at the instruments that show how the engine is functioning. Pilots are taught to scan their instruments every few seconds. With the exception of the fuel gauge, most drivers scan the instruments in their automobiles every few years. That is why so many people find themselves on the freeway with a stopped car, or on a dark street in a strange city, or on the way home from the market. They did not pay attention to information that was provided to them. Their cars did not stop immediately when they stopped paying attention to their instruments, but, eventually, trouble came.

Your body is your vehicle; you are not your body. **You are a soul that is temporarily utilizing your body.** The engine of your vehicle is your energy system. Your emotions continually provide information about how your energy system is functioning. Whether or not you pay attention to this information, your vehicle continues to serve you. Its engine—your energy system—continues to function, unless a problem develops. If a problem occurs, and you are watching how your energy system is functioning, you will spot it immediately.

Your emotions are the instruments that tell you how your energy system is functioning. Scanning the instruments on your energy system means paying attention to your emotions. It means being aware of how energy is being processed at each center. In particular, it means noticing how your body feels in the vicinity of each of these centers at each moment.

THE SCAN

To scan your energy system, begin with a conscious scan of your body from top to bottom. Put your attention at the top of your head, at the seventh center, and let it move down your body to the base of your torso. See what you are feeling in each part of your body. Pay particular attention to what you feel in the vicinity of each center, such as your throat, chest, and stomach. Then do it again.

Practice doing this once a day, then twice a day, and then three times a day, every day. Remembering to scan is the first step. Once you get into the habit, you will look forward to scanning your energy system regularly. The goal is to scan it continually, no matter what you are doing.

Pilots learn to scan their instruments continually while they are flying. They navigate, communicate, and maneuver while they scan the instruments. They consult maps, look at the weather, and discuss flight plans while they scan the instruments. Whatever they do, they scan the instruments while they are doing it.

Scanning your energy system, at each center, mo-

ment by moment, is emotional awareness. Individuals who create authentic power in their lives know how to do this. They notice physical sensations in their bodies, and where they are located. They pay attention to tightness in the right shoulder, pain in the stomach area, heaviness in the chest, or a spasm in the lower back. They do not look at these experiences as chance occurrences. They look at them as information about their energy systems.

Ignoring this information does not cause the vehicle—your body—to fail immediately, but continuing to ignore it will cause a malfunction. A stomach ulcer will develop, or arthritis, or a heart attack. These conditions bring your attention to how your energy system is functioning. If you ignore these signals— your emotions—your energy system will create other physical experiences that are harder, or impossible, to ignore.

That is when you are given time in a hospital to reevaluate your priorities, to be with your vehicle without distractions, and to pay attention to what its instruments are telling you. Paying attention earlier could have accomplished the same thing. In its compassion, the Universe has brought you to a vital awareness of your emotions and the dynamics that produce them. It may be a sickness that appears to be sudden, but **no illness is sudden.** The roots of physical dysfunctions are deep and develop over time.

Emotional awareness gives you the opportunity to make life-changing alterations without the experience of physical dysfunctions to force the issues. It allows you to observe the processing of energy in your energy system, moment by moment, as it occurs, and to detect ways to change them to your benefit. Anger, jealousy, sorrow, greed, vengefulness, and every other form of fear produce destabilizing and energy-draining physical sensations and accompanying thoughts, whether you pay attention to them or try to ignore them. These sensations and thoughts are the read-outs of your instruments.

Gratitude, appreciation, contentment, fulfillment, and joy also produce physical sensations and accompanying thoughts. These sensations and thoughts are nourishing and supportive. They are health-inducing. They balance and reenergize you. Emotional awareness allows you to become aware of, and remain aware of, these experiences, no matter what you are doing, speaking, or thinking, like a pilot who is always aware of what her instruments are telling her.

Think about It

THOUGHTS AND EMOTIONS COME TOGETHER. Most people are not skilled in recognizing this combination. To them, emotions appear to be powerful and uncontrollable. **The more intense an emotion is, the more painful are the sensations in your body and the more compulsive are your thoughts.** You cannot stop hurting and you are fixated on the same thoughts. These intense experiences are what most people think of as anger, jealousy, vengefulness, and so on. In fact, you are always feeling sensations and thinking thoughts.

Sensations always accompany thoughts, and thoughts always accompany sensations. If you are aware only of what you are feeling in your body, you will not be aware of what you are thinking. If you are aware only of what you are thinking, you will not be aware of what you are feeling in your body.

If you were aware of both, you would notice that some sensations in your body occur with particular kinds of thoughts. Patterns would begin to appear, and after a while, you would recognize them. For example, you might find that violent fantasies accompany painful sensations in your stomach area and a tightness in your chest. The reverse is true, too. You might discover that certain types of painful sensations in your stomach

79

area and constrictions in your chest accompany particular types of thoughts.

If you notice one—sensations in your body or your thoughts—and you know what to look for, you will be able to discover the other, too. If you feel a painful sensation in your body, you can observe the type of thought that you are thinking. If you notice the type of thought that you are thinking, you can notice the sensations in your body and where they are.

THINKING ABOUT IT

Do you usually think thoughts and not feel what is going on in your body? Or do you feel your body sensations and are not usually aware of your thoughts? Or are you aware of both? Take time to notice.

Some people are more aware of what they are feeling in their bodies than what they are thinking. Some people are more aware of what they are thinking than what they are feeling in their bodies. Some people think that they do not feel anything. **If you think that you are a person who does not feel anything, or feels very little, think again. Everyone feels physical pain.**

When energy leaves one of the centers in your energy system in fear and doubt, it causes pain in that vicinity. You do not need to feel "emotions" in order to feel this pain. You need only feel the sensations in your body, just as you feel pain in your foot when you stub your toe. Emotional pain is not localized in a finger or a toe. It affects an entire region of your body—your throat (fifth center), chest (fourth center), solar plexus area (third center), and more.

HEAD TO HEART

When you notice that you are thinking and not feeling sensations in your body, move your attention from your head to your heart. Then ask yourself:

"What am I feeling?"

"Where am I having physical sensations in my energy system?"

"What was I avoiding by thinking and not feeling?"

Noticing when energy leaves your energy system in fear and doubt is like noticing when you have a chest cold, a stomachache, or a sore throat. If you do not notice these sensations, it is because you have become accustomed to them. Sight that deteriorates gradually leaves the seer unaware that her ability to see is changing. Eventually, her vision becomes much less sharp than it was at the beginning of the process, but by then, her ability to see less well appears to her as normal. She has nothing to contrast her current visual ability with except how she was able to see yesterday, the week before, and the month before that. From that perspective, there is no change. Yet her vision has deteriorated.

Growing accustomed to painful sensations is a similar process. When the pain is present continually, it begins to appear normal. After a while, it becomes normal. A person who constantly hurts has nothing to contrast his pain with except how he felt yesterday, the week before, and the month before that. From his perspective, he feels no pain. He feels normal. He does not know what it is to live without pain because he has forgotten. He believes that he feels no pain.

Sometimes this happens when parents or peers do not allow the expression of pain. Men teach boys not to express pain, and when the boys become men, they teach boys. Even when expression of physical pain is allowed, the expression of emotional pain usually is not. Women learn the same thing, although in different ways. They are taught not to express themselves to men, and sometimes to other women.

The difference between not feeling pain and believing that you do not feel pain is the difference between being able to enjoy yourself, create freely, and live without fear, and not being able to do these things. People who are in pain laugh now and then. Some of them laugh frequently as a way of denying what they feel. They also enjoy moments of clarity that are free from fear, but they do not live lives characterized by joy, creativity, and fearlessness.

People who think that they feel nothing, especially, are bound by the fears that they think they do not have. They cannot trust other people, themselves, or the Universe. They do not like themselves, and they do not believe they are likable. They are frightened of being who they are, and frightened of others being who they are. They fear that their anger, jealousy, needfulness, or sadness will control them if they allow themselves to feel it. They are damming the rivers of their own lives, and terrified that the dam will break.

If you have grown so accustomed to painful sensations in your body that you are not aware of what your

body is feeling, pay attention to what you are thinking.
A painful sensation in your body that results from energy leaving your energy system in fear and doubt is always accompanied
by a particular kind of thought that compares one situation or
person—including yourself—with another. It sees other people
as things, and judges them.

For example, you might wish that people would understand
you better, or that your job or house were different. You might
think that people who work in certain jobs are not intelligent,
or that people who work in other types of jobs are more worthy
of respect. You might compare groups of people, such as black
people with yellow people, or brown people with white people,
or one woman with another woman, or with men, and so on.

If you have these kinds of thoughts, be aware that at the moment they occur, you are also feeling painful sensations in your
body. If you are not aware of those sensations, begin to look for
them. Move your attention to your chest area, then to your solar
plexus area, or to the lower portions of your torso, or to your
throat. Make the effort to feel what is there. If you feel nothing,
know that painful sensations are there whether you feel them or
not, and keep looking. If your thoughts are judgmental, or you
picture violent fantasies, or wish for what you do not have, they
are there.

If you do not make this effort, these painful sensations will
eventually break through the barriers that you have constructed
and into your awareness in the form of stomach ulcers, throat
cancer, a back pain that will not leave, or any of the numerous
forms of physical dysfunction. There are as many ways to experience painful sensations in your body, and for your body to develop illnesses, as there are ways to judge yourself and others.

Looking for pain that you are feeling when you are not aware of that pain is not the same as creating pain where none exists. Moving your attention to different parts of your body will not create pain. Looking intently for what you are feeling in your body will not create pain. When pain is not there, judgmental thoughts will not be there, either, but if one is present, the other will be, too.

When you are not aware that your body is hurting, you cannot do anything about it. If you do not do anything about it, the cause of the pain will continue. That cause is the release of energy from your energy system in fear and doubt. It is the experience of an individual who fears that she is inadequate and doubts that she should be on the Earth. Her creativity goes into the construction of defenses—against others, against knowing herself, and against Life.

"You care
about life."

When energy leaves your energy system in love and trust, it produces physical sensations of comfort and ease. You are relaxed and your body feels good. Your step is lighter and laughter comes easily. You do not feel painful sensations in your body because there are none. These sensations are accompanied by a particular type of thought, too. You are grateful. You accept. You appreciate. You look for ways to contribute. You care about others. You care about Life. You are in awe of Life, and thankful to be a part of it.

You cannot create a life of fulfillment, joy, and meaning while you are barricading yourself from others and from the opportunities that Life offers you. That is what happens when energy leaves your energy system in fear and doubt.

Think about it.

Connecting the Dots

A PAINFUL EMOTION DOES NOT COME ONCE ONLY, except under a very special circumstance. That circumstance is when you recognize the emotion the first time it comes, discover what causes it, and change it. Otherwise, an emotion returns again and again. That is what makes it familiar.

You may not enjoy your sadness, anger, or jealousy, but they are not new experiences. Neither is greed, fear that you have done something wrong, feeling that people do not understand you, or any of the many ways that painful physical sensations and tormenting thoughts combine. Your experiences of anger, jealousy, greed, and other forms of fear are unique to you. **Energy leaves your energy system in ways that are specific to you, and that release of energy is accompanied by thoughts that are particular to you, too.**

Fingerprints are unique and identifiable. Once your fingerprints are on record, that record can be matched with your fingerprints wherever they appear. When the match is made, you are identified precisely.

The same thing is true of emotions. Each emotion that you experience is unique. **Once you identify an emotion, you will be able to recognize it whenever it appears.** If you are not able to identify it precisely, you will not be able to make a perfect match when it appears again, and you will think that every angry experience you have, for example, is different. It is not. The circumstances that appear to trigger your anger may change, but your anger does not. You might become angry at your neighbor one time, and at your classmate another. You might be jealous of your partner one time, and later in your life become jealous of another partner. The partners are not the same, but your jealousy is.

The more familiar you become with your emotions, the more easily you will be able to see how they remain the same, even though the circumstances in which they appear change. The sadness you feel now is the same sadness you have felt before. The anger, jealousy, vengefulness, and greed are also the same emotions you have felt before. You may think that the emotion you are experiencing is similar, but not identical, to an emotion you experienced before, but that is because you did not take the time to study the emotion thoroughly when it appeared earlier.

You can start examining your emotions at any time. The best time to start is now. The sooner you begin to look closely at what you are feeling in your body and what you are thinking at the same time, the sooner you will begin to identify emotions that repeat themselves. Eventually you will see that they all do.

Take the time to make a note of what you are thinking when you notice a painful sensation in your solar plexus area, or in your chest, or a constriction in your throat. Do the opposite, too. Write down what you are feeling in your body when you notice that you are comparing people or things—when you are judging what is good and bad, useful and useless, courageous and cowardly, intelligent and stupid, compassionate and cruel, and so on. You will soon find that you have a lot of notes because you are continually feeling sensations in your body and thinking thoughts.

As you practice putting your sensations and your thoughts together, you will recognize repeating combinations. Eventually, those combinations will become more familiar, and you will know at a glance which one has come. When you are angry because you feel that you have been deliberately wronged, for example, you may feel a pain in your chest area (fourth center) and a different kind of pain in your solar plexus areas (third center). When you are angry because you think someone has acted unintelligently, or thoughtlessly, you may feel painful sensations in the same two areas, but different kinds of painful sensations.

Most people feel painful sensations in those two areas when they are angry, but only you will feel the particular sensations that you do, in exactly the places and ways that you do. They, and the thoughts that accompany them, are your fingerprint. You have ten fingerprints on your hands. All your fingerprints together identify you even more unmistakably than the print from a single finger.

You have many, many more emotional fingerprints. All of the different sensations in the vicinities of all of the different centers in your energy system, all of the thoughts that you think when they occur, and the combinations of all of the sensations, locations, and thoughts is much more complex than any collection of prints from your fingers. That is why you will have so many notes when you begin to observe what you are feeling at the same time that you think judgmental thoughts. The number of possible ways to feel painful sensations and to judge others is very large, and the number of combinations is even larger.

In short, your emotional landscape is very rich. Walking through it without paying attention to what is there is like walking through a meadow without paying attention to what is growing. You can see that the meadow is colorful in the spring, green in the summer, and brown in the fall, but you do not know what flowers or grass grow there. When you look closely, you see red, purple, yellow, white, and blue flowers. When you look even more closely, you see that the purple flowers have six petals, the white flowers are larger, the red flowers grow along their stalks, and so on. The closer you look, the more you see.

When you study the meadow long enough, you also see the insects, birds, and animals that live there. If you return to the meadow often, and look closely at it each time, you will eventually become very familiar with it. It will still be beautiful. It will still change with the seasons, but you will be able to appreciate it much more because you know it so intimately.

Before you become aware of your emotional landscape, all you see are the intense emotions that grip your attention now and then. You know when you are enraged, upset, or very happy. There is much more to see, just as there is more to see in a meadow than different colors. When you know

"The closer you look,
the more you see—"

your emotional landscape as well as you know a meadow where every kind of flower, insect, bird, and animal is familiar to you, you will recognize each of the painful sensations in your body and the thoughts that you think at the same time just as easily.

If you start paying attention to your emotions now, you will be able to see when the emotions that you experience this week occur again, and then again, and then again. You do not have to stop there. You can also look for times in the past when you experienced those emotions. The more you open yourself to this type of inquiry, the more occasions you will remember. For example, you might remember being angry with your father when you were five years old because he came into your room without knocking. You might remember being angry with your roommate in school because he opened your closet without your permission. You might also remember becoming angry with your partner last week because she read your mail without asking you if she could.

If you look at each of these experiences as separate events, they appear as dots on a piece of paper. Each stands alone. When you look at all of them as a single experience that is extended in time, you connect the dots. You see a line that begins with anger at your father, continues through anger with your roommate, and ends with anger at your partner.

You will also see that these experiences have something in common. In each instance, you felt that your privacy was not respected. In each case, you felt violated. The people you were angry with changed, but the reason you became angry did not change, and neither did the anger you felt. Each time it caused the same painful sensations in your body.

CONNECTING THE DOTS

1. Remember something that upset you today or recently. Remember something that made you angry or that you reacted to strongly. Picture that person or situation clearly in your mind. What emotions did you feel? What thoughts were you having and where did you feel the physical sensations in your body? Can you recognize what energy locations were affected?

2. Think of a time that something similar happened. Go through the same questions for this situation. What emotions did you feel? What thoughts were you having and where did you feel the physical sensations in your body? Can you recognize what energy locations were affected?

3. Do it again—remember a time, perhaps when you were a child, when similar feelings and thoughts occurred. Answer the same questions again. What emotions did you feel? What thoughts were you having and where did you feel the physical sensations in your body? Can you recognize what energy locations were affected?

Now connect the dots. See if you can identify the same physical sensations and types of thoughts in each circumstance. That is plotting the map of your emotional landscape.

The purpose of connecting the dots is not to determine where and when your anger began but to familiarize you with your emotional landscape. Recognizing that you get angry now and then is like walking through the meadow and noticing red flowers in it. Becoming familiar enough with your anger to know how it feels each time it occurs, what kinds of thoughts you think each time it occurs, and when it happened in the past is like walking through the meadow and knowing all of the red flowers in it, how they are shaped, their fragrance, and the texture of their petals.

"...*plotting the map of your emotional landscape.*"

There are other emotions in your emotional landscape, too, just as there are other kinds of flowers in the meadow. As you become familiar with each of them, your appreciation of your emotional landscape increases in the same way that your appreciation of the meadow increases when you become aware of everything in it.

After you live in a house for a few years, you become so familiar with it that you always know where you are in it, even in the dark. When you live in a neighborhood a long time, especially one you have explored a lot, you become so familiar with it that you cannot get lost.

When you become that familiar with your emotional landscape, you will never get lost in it, either.

The Present Moment

YOU ARE ALWAYS IN THE PRESENT MOMENT. You are not always aware that you are in the present moment. The present moment continues with your awareness or without it. The difference is one of power. When you are aware in the present moment, you have the option of power. **When you are not aware in the present moment, you have no power.**

Not having power means being under the control of external circumstances. Having the option to create power means you are able to decide what you will say next and do next, and the consequences you will create with your words and actions. All possibilities exist in the present moment. **When you are aware of the present moment, you have access to all possibilities that the present moment offers.**

Most people are not aware of the present moment, and the options available to them are very limited. When they are offended, they get angry and shout or withdraw. When they are tempted by alcohol, they drink it. When they are jealous, they become focused on a narrow part of the vast array of experience that presents itself moment by moment.

That vast array is all contained in the present moment. Becoming aware of the present moment gives access to that vast array, and with that vast array of experience comes numerous possibilities.

It is not possible to become aware of the present moment by examining, studying, or thinking about external circumstances. The more absorbed you become in these activities, the less aware of the present moment you are. When you are fixated on your computer, for example, time seems to go by very quickly and you don't have enough of it. Before you are finished with what you want to do, dinner is ready, or it is bedtime, and you stay up late to do even more.

The same is true of homework, business demands, and every other activity that takes you away from the present moment. You put on blinders, and it is not possible to distract you because you are like a train on tracks. All you see are the tracks unfolding before you, and none of the landscape that continually presents itself.

You cannot see all of the outer landscape that surrounds you while you are unaware of you inner landscape. Your inner landscape is the anchor of your experience. It is the ground of your life. When you live your life without seeing it, your life becomes ungrounded. You are tossed about by circumstances like a leaf in the wind. You become a boat without a rudder, and the currents of your life take you where they go, whether you want to go there or not.

Your inner landscape is richer than your outer landscape, no matter how magnificent the sunrise you are seeing might be, or how awesome the night sky above you, or how immense the turbulent ocean rushing toward you. It is more diverse and more meaningful. It is your inner landscape that gives meaning to your outer landscape. A golden sunset does not fill you with appreciation. Your inner

*"Your inner landscape
is richer..."*

landscape does. When you mistake the circumstances that you
encounter in your outer landscape for the experiences of your
inner landscape, you miss the point entirely.

The point is that you are on the Earth in order to grow spiritually and to give gifts that only you are capable of giving.
Those gifts do not originate in the outer world but in the deepest parts of yourself. They are your potential waiting to spring
into being like seeds in the Earth waiting to sprout. Your
"earth" is your inner landscape. The more attention you pay to
it, the more familiar you become with it, and the more familiar
you become with it, the more able you are to see what you want
to cultivate and what you want to remove.

Your inner landscape is always changing. You may be content for a few moments, then angry, then jealous, then delighted,
and then angry again. Throughout your life, your inner landscape presents itself to you again and again. This presentation
continues until you die—until your soul goes home.

Only you can change the contents of that presentation, and
only after you become aware of what it is. Then you can observe it as it flows through you. When you are not aware of it,
your emotions delight you, disturb you, calm you, and agitate
you. They frighten you, please you, and confuse you.

Your emotions are the force field of your soul, not products of hormones, enzymes, and neurotransmitters. They are the experiences, coming to you in a dramatically intimate way, of parts of your soul. **Painful emotions—such as anger, fear, jealousy, and vengefulness—are experiences of the parts of your soul that your soul desires to heal.** Emotions that nurture you, such as gratitude, contentment, and appreciation, are experiences of the parts of your soul that are already healthy.

When you are aware of everything that you are feeling, all the time, you are in continual communication with your soul. Learning how to listen to that communication, and act on it, is the purpose of your being in the Earth school. Becoming aware of your soul does not require isolation, a special diet, or meditation. It does not require that you study or take examinations. It begins with your becoming aware of what you are feeling. It requires recognizing everything that you are feeling moment by moment—how your energy system is processing the energy moving through it.

This communication with your soul can be very difficult to listen to, and sometimes it is extremely painful. In those cases especially, it is easier to run away from the communication than to remain and hear it. When your stomach is hurting, or your chest is aching, or both are in pain, it is difficult to listen to what your soul is saying. That is when most people shout at someone else, or at a pet, or throw a dish, or withdraw in resentment, hit a pillow, decide to get divorced, or go shopping, turn on the television, eat, or in some other way divert their attention.

The more painful the communication is, the more compulsive is the desire to avoid the communication. There are fundamentally two ways to avoid experiencing what you are feeling. The first is to escape into your thoughts.

People judge one another because it is easier to believe that someone else is responsible for their circumstances than it is to face the pain of their circumstances or the reality of the world around them. This flight into thoughts is the same as putting a numbing agent on a wound. The wound does not disappear. It must still be treated. Nothing has changed except that, for the moment, you do not feel it. When the numbing agent wears off, the wound is there, and so is the pain.

LOST IN THOUGHT

Give yourself some time to explore whether you avoid listening to the communication with your soul—feeling your emotions—by escaping into thoughts.

Do you think about things that have happened to you and wish they were different?

Do you spend time planning for the future, or dreading it?

Do you occupy yourself with the what ifs of your life?

If the answer to these questions is yes, allow at least five minutes each morning and five minutes each evening to listen to the communications with your soul—to feel what you are feeling, and where you are feeling it, in your energy system.

When the pain of communication with your soul becomes intense, you are at a pivotal moment. The choice that confronts you is whether to ease the pain you feel by escaping from it into thoughts or activities, or to keep your attention inward in order to learn where your discomfort is coming from, and heal the source of it. Becoming immersed in circumstances around you is the decision to pursue external power. **Remaining with your inner experience is the choice to pursue authentic power.**

Emotions, Power, and the Present Moment

EMOTIONAL PAIN IS PHYSICAL PAIN. Your body hurts, sometimes intensely. As you become aware of what you are feeling, you become aware of this pain when it comes. Do not worry about what emotions you are feeling. Direct your attention to what your body feels. Its experiences are the emotions you are looking for.

Scan the locations in your energy system. Notice what your body is experiencing, and where, using your knowledge of your energy system to guide you. Is your chest area (fourth center) tight? What do you feel in the area around your solar plexus (third center)? Is your voice (fifth center) full and rich, or choked and weak? Are your neck and shoulders tight? Directing your attention in this way is the first step in the creation of authentic power.

When you direct your attention elsewhere, you miss your emotions. You see yourself in the past or in the future. You think about what you could have done, or what you will do. You dwell on what others did, or will do. You think about how things will be or could be.

Each thought is accompanied by emotions, but if you are not willing to examine what your body is experiencing in the moment, you will divert yourself again and again into more and more thoughts, ideas, plans, calculations, and judgments. Entire domains of intellectual activity have been created in order to divert the attention of those who created them from emotions they do not wish to feel. Intellectual endeavor and emotional awareness are not mutually exclusive, but when an intellectual pursuit becomes compulsive, it is being used to divert attention from painful emotions.

MORE THAN A LABEL

Pick a time in your life when you had a painful emotional experience, for example, a boyfriend or girlfriend left you, a parent or someone close to you died, or you got fired. Go back to that time in your imagination. Remember how you felt. How would you describe your feelings (for example, sad, jealous, angry)? Really let yourself feel what you felt at the time. Give yourself a minute or two. Notice where in your body you are feeling physical sensations. (If you are not used to feeling the physical sensations in your body—your energy system—be patient).

Feel where in your energy system you are feeling physical sensations or discomfort. Doing this practice will help you connect the emotions (anger, sadness, jealousy) to where you are feeling physical sensations of discomfort in your energy system.

The second way to avoid painful emotions is to escape into an activity. It is easier to create a business, become an honor student or a varsity player than it is to experience the intense physical pain of a painful emotion. It is easier to become the best salesperson in the company, the hardest worker, or the most brilliant problem solver. Computer games, television, and making money divert attention from painful emotions. Any activity can—including eating, shopping, drinking, and sex. Climbing ladders—social, economic, or military—diverts attention from painful emotions.

When an activity is used to divert attention from painful emotions, it is compulsive. The idea of coming to the end of a prolonged project, such as remodeling a house, a business, or a career, is naturally appealing, especially if the project has been difficult. When the activity is a diversion from emotional pain, the approach of the conclusion of the activity is frightening. The activity conceals a need, and when the activity is concluded the need reappears, just as pain from an anesthetized wound reappears when the anesthetic wears off.

Look at the activities in your life and see which ones are compulsive. You hurt when you stop doing compulsive activities before you are exhausted by them—whether that is fixing a computer, painting a room, or growing a garden. If you complete a compulsive project before you are exhausted, you will find another activity to begin. A compulsive activity does not unfold in its own time. You push it. You do not want to be distracted from it because it prevents you from experiencing what your body is feeling, and what you are thinking.

Compulsion is not the same as passion. **Passion is the unfolding of joy.** It opens possibilities. It creates and contributes. **Compulsion is the unfolding of fear.** It closes possibilities and perceptions and it excludes. It fixates the one who is compulsive. The difference between the joy of Life and the obsession to finish a project is the difference between freedom and imprisonment. The prison is a fortress that has been constructed to keep emotions out. It also keeps the prisoner in. Leaving the prison is a life-changing experience. The compulsion to compete and win gives way to the desire to belong and contribute. Fear is replaced by gratitude. Self-concern becomes care for others and the Earth.

PASSION OR COMPULSION

Make a list of your daily activities, including your leisure activities. For each activity, ask yourself the following questions and write down your answers:

"Does it unfold in its own time or do I push it?"

"Does it open possibilities or close them?"

"Does it open perceptions or close them?"

"Am I avoiding my emotions or welcoming them?"

"Is this an unfolding of joy or an unfolding of fear?"

"Am I only self-concerned or do I care for others and the Earth?"

"Is this a passion or a diversion?"

The first step in uncovering the origin of a compulsion is the hardest. **To uncover the origin of a compulsion, you must stop doing what is compulsive and experience what you feel when you do.** If you flee back into an activity or your thoughts, be gentle with yourself. Your wholeness is greater than you can imagine. It is worth the effort and the time required to uncover it. If the intensity of a painful emotion is more than you can endure without striking out at another person, complaining of an injustice, blaming someone or yourself, or withdrawing or dominating, try to experience it for one minute without distracting yourself.

The next time the pain of rage, or of feeling inferior, feeling superior, jealousy, vengefulness, or greed comes, try to experience it without distraction for two minutes. Learn how to swim before you jump into the deep water. The waters of your soul are very deep. You were born to immerse yourself in them. Do that consciously. Emotional awareness is the first step.

If you are not aware of what you are feeling in your body and what you are thinking, you are not aware of the present moment. You have no power. You are occupied with what is in front of you, and only a small portion of that. You are unaware of what others are feeling and how they are behaving, except when their behaviors affect you. Most important, you are unaware of yourself. You have no memory of yourself as a soul, as an influence on others, of your contract with the Universe or the breadth and scope of your creative capacity. Becoming conscious of these things requires that you become aware of your emotions.

When you are not aware of your emotions, your attention is focused on the circumstances around you. The major element in your experience will remain invisible to you—the emotions that continually move through you. As long as you do not know what you are experiencing inside, you are asleep to your life, even though you may think that you are very much awake.

Scientists call something that is necessary to an outcome, but by itself is not enough, "necessary but not sufficient." Emotional awareness is necessary but not sufficient to becoming aware of the present moment. Without emotional awareness, you cannot be aware of the present moment because the present moment contains your emotions. However, many people are so much aware of their emotions they are overwhelmed by them. They cry or laugh uncontrollably. They are swept away by their fear, jealousy, rage, joy, or sorrow. When that happens, they are aware of little, or nothing, else.

Whenever your attention is fixated, you are aware only of the object of your fixation. That object can be an external circumstance—such as a career opportunity, the death of a friend, the creation of a business, passing a class in school, cooking a meal, or washing a car. It can also be an emotion. In both cases, you remain unaware of the present moment. You forget who you are and where you are. You also forget what you are and why you are.

Emotional awareness is the healing remedy for a fixation on external circumstances. As you become aware of everything you are feeling, the experiences of your life transform from black-and-white (when you see only what is outside of you) to color (when you become aware of what is inside of you at the same time). However, if you are aware only of what is inside of you, you are as fixated as an individual who cannot see beyond his job or her need for a mate.

The healing remedy for a fixation on what you are experiencing inside of you is something else. Without that something else, you will not experience emotional awareness. You will experience only emotional involvement.

With that something else, you will not only become emotionally aware, you will step into the eternal present moment.

Detachment

IMAGINE GOING TO A MOVIE that has won nine academy awards, including best actor, best actress, best director, best cinematography, and best musical score. It is your favorite kind of movie, and your favorite actress and actor play the leading roles. The screenplay is superb and you are fascinated from the moment the opening scene begins, to the very end, with its beautiful closing music.

You exit the theater still thinking about what you have experienced, and discover that it is raining outside, or sunny, or windy. Until then, you forgot completely about everything except the movie. It was an experience unto itself. Its effect on you was so powerful that you forgot where you were, what you were doing before you came, and what you planned to do afterward. You were unaware of the people in the theater with you and of the employees in the theater selling tickets to the next performance, popping corn, and cleaning the lobby. You were unaware of your job, your school, and your friends.

That is what it is like to be fixated on the events of your life. You forget everything else. **When you are fixated on the events of your life, your attention is absorbed.** The circumstances around you make you laugh and cry. You know when you are laughing and crying, but the laughter and tears happen without your noticing much about them. You are focused on what you think caused them.

Now imagine going to the movie with someone who is very attractive to you. You might have felt this way the first time you went out with your first girlfriend or boyfriend. Perhaps you felt this way when you first discovered that you wanted to marry your wife or your husband.

The movie is no longer what you notice. You are aware of your friend. You notice when she moves. You are aware of when his arm touches yours. You feel each other's presence throughout the movie. You do not forget about each other, no matter how exciting the movie becomes. You are the center of each other's attention.

Now you have become absorbed in another movie—the one with your friend. This movie will not end when you leave the theater. It has a constantly changing cast. The characters do unexpected things, and those things affect you in ways that make you laugh and cry. While you are absorbed in this movie, you are not aware of yourself any more than when you were absorbed with your favorite actor and actress.

You are again in a movie with your favorite actor—this time one who is always at the center of the action and has no understudy. That is you. When you were absorbed in the movie at the theater, you forgot that you were in the theater. While you are absorbed in the external circumstances of your life, such as your friend, you forget that you are in a much larger learning arena. That is the Earth school. You also forget that you have things to learn in the Earth school, and that your experiences are your learning opportunities.

If the lights suddenly came on in the theater while you were absorbed in the movie, you would awaken to the reality of the theater and the people around you. You would continue to see the movie on the screen in front of you, and, at the same time, you would see the inside of the theater, the rows of seats, the people in them and what they are doing. You would see popcorn on the floor, the color of the walls, and the speakers that make the movie sound so real.

If the lights suddenly came on inside you while you were absorbed in the larger movie that is the external circumstances of your life, you would continue to see that larger movie and you would also become aware of your interior circumstances. You would see your outer landscape and your inner landscape at the same time, just as you were able to see the movie on the screen and the interior of the theater at the same time when the lights came on. You would make connections between your emotions (your inner landscape) and what is happening around you (your outer landscape), and between your thoughts (also parts of your inner landscape) and what is happening around you. All of these would be part of the same picture, and you would see the entire picture.

Your inner and outer landscapes would both be part of your experience. The argument with your friend and your reactions

"...you would see
the entire picture."

to your friend, the beauty of the child you admire and the experience of your admiration, the complexity of the project that you completed and the satisfaction of completing it—all of what you experience would be present in your awareness. That is awareness of the present moment.

Awareness of the present moment requires detachment from both your outer landscape and your inner landscape. Until you become aware of your inner and outer landscapes, you cannot view them at all, much less with detachment. When you become aware of your outer landscape, but you are not detached from it, you are absorbed in what is occurring around you, and you are unable to experience your emotions. When you become aware of your inner landscape but are not detached from it, you are absorbed in your emotions, and you are unable to step back from them long enough to see them clearly.

Work on moving one step back from what you are feeling so you are no longer blinded by it or unaware of it as a feeling. Move one step away so you can let it begin to work its way through you without penetrating as deeply as it does in terms of creating action and negative thoughts and emotional withdrawals and all the other reactions it has created within you in the past. Become one step detached from what you are feeling, and every time you are able to, you will become more and more and more detached.

The difference between being detached from your emotions and being swept away by them is the difference between standing on a bridge looking down on rushing water below you and being in the water.

When you are in the water, you can see only a little of it—

the water that is around you. When you are angry, for example, you can only experience your anger. When you are on the bridge, you can see the stream—you can see your anger approach, rush under the bridge, and move downstream as jealousy approaches, rushes under the bridge, and is replaced by a feeling of inferiority, and so on. That is detachment.

ON THE BRIDGE

Use this practice when you are feeling any painful emotion, such as anger, jealousy, sadness, depression, vengefulness, or greed. Imagine that you are in a river of these emotions. Now imagine yourself getting out of the water and walking out onto a bridge. You look down at the river and watch it rushing below you. The water in the river represents your emotions. Let this water flow below you while you watch. At the same time feel the river of energy flowing through your body. Allow yourself to feel these emotions with detachment, like watching the river flow below you while you are on the bridge.

Practice this each time you are caught in a river of emotions.

*"...you can see the river
of your emotions..."*

Detachment allows you to remain aware of what you feel while the events of your life unfold. When you are detached, your emotions run through you like water through a hose. You are the hose. The same water does not stay in the same place in a hose when the faucet is turned on. Your emotional faucet is never turned off. The fear, resentment, anger, depression, contentment, jealousy, rage, or joy that you feel do not stay, either. When you look at your emotions in this way you can detach from them enough that you will not be controlled by them.

When you can do that, your emotions run off you like water in a shower. You do not absorb your emotions any more than a duck absorbs water running off its feathers. **When you are not detached from your emotions, you cannot separate yourself from them and they possess you.** You strike out, withdraw, or shout. You fester in resentment or laugh uncontrollably.

This shower never stops, and you are always in it. Your changing emotions are your continual experiences of the different ways energy is being processed at different locations in your energy system. **When you become aware of your emotions, you are in a position to change how the energy moving through your energy system is processed.** Your emotions no longer sweep you away. They inform you and provide you with important data. You cannot receive this information and be submerged in your emotions at the same time—you cannot become aware of what your body is feeling when you are angry, for example, and shout in anger at the same time.

You must choose between being in the water and letting your emotions determine your words and actions, and standing on the bridge watching your anger as it moves painfully through you. When you are in the water, your anger is your master, and it controls what you do. When you stand on the bridge and experience your anger, no matter how painful the sensations in your body are, you are the master of your anger, and you control what you do. Each time you do this, your anger loses power over you and you gain power over it. This is how authentic power is created.

When you are aware of your emotions and what is occurring around you, you step into the present moment. You take up residence in your mansion. The owner is in. The driver is awake at the wheel. All of the experiences of your life are designed to assist your movement into this position.

Intimacy

NTIMACY IS THE MEASURE OF THE ENERGY that leaves your energy system in love and trust. Lack of intimacy is the measure of the energy that leaves your energy system in fear and doubt. Intimacy and the lack of intimacy appear to be accidental experiences when you are not aware of your energy system and how it is working.

When you are aware of your energy system and you know how it works, you can create intimacy when you choose. Intimacy does not mean a close relationship with another individual, although that can happen when you experience intimacy. It also does not mean that others act in one particular way toward you or another. **The experience of intimacy is not related to how others act or do not act, or how they speak or do not speak. It depends upon how energy leaves your energy system.**

When energy leaves your processing system in love and trust, the result is the experience of intimacy. When it leaves in fear and doubt, the result is the opposite experience. You feel isolated and separate. These two experiences are easy to recognize. The first, intimacy, is gratifying and joyful. You feel open to your life and to others. You look forward to being with others. You care about them. You feel connected to them, even if they do not feel connected to you. You are interested in them.

You appreciate them, and you appreciate that they are in your life.

> ### THINK OF A TIME
>
> **Think of a time when you felt close to someone or a group of people. Perhaps it was at a family gathering where the truth was being told, or when someone was dying and everyone was feeling so sad and also feeling so close, or at a community tragedy that brought people in the community closer together. At these times there is a feeling of intimacy. This is a group experience of energy leaving each person in love and trust.**
>
> **Remember how you felt—the love you felt for each person no matter what your past experiences were, the tenderness you felt for the people with you, and the warm, glowing feelings in your body. Remember that feeling—most of your energy was leaving your body in love and trust in those moments.**

The second experience, lack of intimacy, is painful. People appear to you as objects. You are not interested in what they are feeling or thinking, except when it affects you. You are more concerned with things, such as a new car or a better job, than you are with people. Activities, such as finishing a project or achieving a goal, are more important to you than people. Everything is more important to you than people, unless you need them to accomplish what you want.

Intimacy requires vulnerability. Being vulnerable does not require that you share every feeling of insecurity you have with another person, or with anyone. It requires that you feel your every experience of insecurity. If you cannot feel your own insecurities, you will not be able to see them in others, much less appreciate them in others. Intimacy creates sensitivity. When you are intimate you become sensitive to yourself and also to other people. When you are not intimate, you are sensitive only to yourself, and even then you are not aware of everything that you are feeling.

AM I SENSITIVE?

Are you truly sensitive, or are you too sensitive? Ask yourself, "Am I . . ."

Truly Sensitive		Too Sensitive
Aware of other people's feelings?	Or	Taking things personally?
Responsive to other people?	Or	Reactive to other people?
Seeing the situation clearly?	Or	Judging the circumstances?
Interested in myself and others?	Or	Only interested in myself?

Intimacy is natural for us. We long to experience intimacy, and we are designed to be intimate—caring, sensitive, and loving toward one another. When you are intimate, you are fulfilled. Every encounter is satisfying, or pregnant with potential for deeper insight and spiritual growth. When you are not caring, sensitive, or loving—when intimacy is lacking—nothing fulfills. Every interaction is cold, and sometimes cruel. Vulnerability is dangerous. This is a very painful experience. You feel isolated and alone. You cannot reach others and they cannot reach you. You strive to accomplish activities and achieve goals rather than create relationships. The only relationships you seek are functional—those that help you obtain what you desire.

Intimacy and the pursuit of external power—the ability to manipulate and control—are incompatible. Where one exists the other cannot exist. Lack of intimacy and the pursuit of authentic power—the alignment of the personality with the soul—are also mutually exclusive. **When you naturally create harmony, cooperation, sharing, and reverence for Life, you cannot suffer from lack of intimacy.**

When projects, accomplishments, and goals become more important to you than people, you walk into a cold, dark room, like a large refrigerator. Your life becomes this room. Everywhere you go is cold. No one appears supportive to you, even if that is his or her intention, because your intention toward him or her is not warm or supportive. You cannot imagine in others what you cannot experience in yourself, so you walk in loneliness, no matter how many friends approach you. You dismiss compliments as flattery and disdain appreciation as ignorance. There is a wall between you and others as real as a wall made of concrete and steel.

That wall also separates you from much of what you are feeling. Your awareness is limited to your anger, frustration, and disappointment. You are aware of the ways individuals do not meet your expectations, of your judgments of others and yourself. Deeper, more painful emotions remain invisible to you. **When you do not recognize your deeper, painful emotions for what they are, they shape your perceptions, judgments, and actions.**

Chief among these emotions is fear. It is easier to become angry than to experience that you are frightened. Fear and hopelessness come together. You see your circumstance as beyond your ability to alter, or you would not be frightened. Anger is an attempt to change others so that you feel more secure. The more frightened you are, the more righteous you become, and the more others appear to be at fault. You feel justified in your anger, because your judgments are anchored in a reality that you have constructed.

All painful emotions are expressions of fear. When you are caught in a current of rage or remorse, or seek revenge, you cannot see that. You see only a cause of your anger, a loss that you cannot replace or an injustice that torments you. As you strike out in anger, withdraw in sorrow, or seethe at an injustice, you keep yourself from the central perception of what lies at the root of your pain. That is fear.

All you see around you, everyone you encounter, and all you experience inwardly are reflections of a fear that permeates your awareness. Until you can turn to face your own fears, you will be a prisoner of them. You will not find your way out of the cold, dark room. You will not even know that there is an outside. Your life will be filled with anger, vengefulness, regret, envy, and more. This is the experience of no intimacy, a painful descent into powerlessness.

FACE YOUR FEARS

For one day experiment with noticing every painful emotion you have. Notice what physical sensations you are having and where they are in your energy system. Remember that all painful emotions are expressions of fear—such as anger, jealousy, sadness, vengefulness, and greed—they are emotions that come with thoughts of judging yourself and others.

Some individuals do not know another type of experience. They see others as ~~threats, opportunities,~~ targets, resources, or the answers to their prayers. This is the human condition that is now undergoing transition. Intimacy is not the perception of immediate family, close friends, or dearest relatives as allies, sources of strength, and shelters against the storms that blow. **Intimacy is trusting that the Universe will provide what you need, when you need it, and in the manner most appropriate for you.**

The transformation that is reshaping the human experience is introducing millions of individuals to the possibility of intimacy and providing glimpses of a way of being that makes all others unsatisfactory. It is the intuition that a difficult situation has meaning for you. It is the sudden moment of empathy with someone who previously seemed repugnant. It is the insight into the fears, struggles, and joys of another. It is melting into your own humanity.

Intimacy is letting your guard down. You relax into the present moment without reservation. You become a friend to the world, and the world becomes a friend to you. You welcome every circumstance instead of resisting it. You face forward into the wind. The wind is the force of your life shaping itself to meet your most fundamental needs—the needs of your soul.

Every circumstance becomes a gift—the friend who assists you, the neighbor who deceives you, the stranger who smiles, kind people and brutal people, individuals who meet your expectations and individuals who do not. All provide you with opportunities to explore yourself, discover more about yourself, and change yourself. The issue is never about another individual. It is always about you. The question is not how to change other people. It is how to change yourself so that you do not re-live the same painful experiences.

> **WHEN I BRING INTIMACY INTO MY LIFE**
>
> **I become a friend to the world and the world is a friend to me.**
>
> **I welcome every circumstance instead of resisting it.**
>
> **Energy leaves my energy system in love and trust.**
>
> **I appreciate myself and others.**

When you look at your life in this way, you transcend the contents of your life. You no longer focus on what makes you angry, but on the experience of anger in yourself. You no longer direct your attention to what frustrates you, but to the excruciating experience of frustration. Instead of blaming others, shouting at others, judging others, withdrawing from others, or the many other ways of attempting to manipulate others, you look inward at the roots of the painful emotions that generate these behaviors.

You are no longer content to behave in a way that merely covers over, or avoids, a painful emotion that has controlled you in the past. You become a fearless explorer of your own inner terrain. There you delight in all that you discover, including your fears and the particular ways they come to you. These are some of the many combinations of ways energy is processed in your energy system. Your joy, gratitude, and love, which are boundless, are also combinations of ways energy is processed in your energy system.

When you change the question from
"How can I change others?"
to
"How can I change myself?"
you consciously enter the Earth school.
You focus on the experience of painful emotions
that are happening inside you
and
not what is happening outside of you.
You focus on . . .

The experience of anger in yourself	*Not*	*What makes you angry*
The experience of jealousy in yourself	*Not*	*What makes you jealous*
The experience of sadness in yourself	*Not*	*What makes you sad*
The experience of fear in yourself	*Not*	*What frightens you*

And on and on.

You no longer run from your life and yourself. You welcome both as friends on the journey of your soul that began with your birth into the Earth school and will end at the death of your personality—when your soul goes home. Between these two events you encounter the circumstances of your life and respond to them. Each time you respond, you create more circumstances. Each of them offers you the opportunity to look at yourself, not others, and change—yourself, not others.

You are committed to your own spiritual growth more than to the accomplishment of your projects, more than to making your life the way you think it should be, and more than to making the world the way you think it should be. You reshape the world by reshaping yourself. You see the world and all that is in it as being at the service of your soul. This is an accurate perception. It is the perception of your experiences and the circumstances of your life as the continually updated curricula of the Earth school. All that you encounter is your teacher, and you are the student.

The objective of the Earth school
is to assist you in learning
how to create
AUTHENTIC POWER.
To inhabit the Earth with the
perceptions
values
and
goals
of your soul.
They are
HARMONY
COOPERATION
SHARING
REVERENCE FOR LIFE.

Your teacher is very patient. If you do not learn what your circumstances seek to teach you, more circumstances arrive to help you learn the same lesson. This continues as long as necessary—for years, for a lifetime, or for lifetimes. When you become interested in the curricula of the Earth school, your life becomes very interesting.

You no longer look at your endeavors as successes and failures. You do not judge yourself or others. You know we are all fellow students in the same school. This is intimacy. You have no enemies, only fellow students in the Earth school. You have no successes or failures, only the consequences of experiments in the use of your will—which means in the creation of your experiences. You cannot fail the course. No one can. It is only a matter of how you approach your studies.

"You cannot fail
the course,
No one can."

While you remain locked in anger, jealousy, vengefulness, and the other forms of fear, you cannot see the opportunities your life presents to you. You cannot face the deeper, more painful experiences of fear and powerlessness, and so more opportunities come to you until you do. When your life begins to change, you lose interest in changing others. **You create intimacy when you shift from the pursuit of external power—the ability to manipulate and control—to the pursuit of authentic power—the alignment of your personality with your soul.**

This is intimacy.

PART II

Running Away

Soul View

LOOK AT YOURSELF as a student in the Earth school. In this school you are continually given opportunities to discover your emotional dynamics and learn about them. You have preexisting inclinations toward certain experiences under certain conditions. These inclinations are patterns of emotional response that exist independently of the circumstances that activate them.

Your study assignment in the Earth school is to keep focused on these emotional patterns as they become active and while they are active. You cannot do this while you are focused on the circumstances that bring them to life. Those circumstances are merely triggers that put into motion the patterns of response that you experience as emotions.

When you turn your attention inward to these patterns of emotional response, you begin to see that the same painful emotions occur in you again and again, although the triggers that activate them are different. It is the emotional response—not the trigger—that remains the same.

Removing the trigger does not solve the problem. The pattern remains in place. **Most people use their energy attempting to rearrange circumstances that trigger painful emotions.** They change jobs, friends, and spouses. They choose new careers and houses. **Changing external circumstances will not change your rigid patterns of emotional response.** That requires looking at the patterns themselves.

This section provides you with in-depth examinations of some ways people avoid the experience of their emotions. Each of them diverts attention and redirects it outward toward people, circumstances, and activities. They are also ways of avoiding the healing that is necessary to permanently eliminate painful emotions, just as a child finds ways to avoid taking a medicine she does not like.

The medicine that your life offers you is your emotions. Using that medicine requires becoming intimately aware of your emotions—of the physical sensations that occur in your body and the thoughts that accompany them. In other words, paying attention to your energy system moment by moment is the healing medicine.

In this section you will find ways of avoiding emotions that you recognize in yourself, and also ways that you think do not apply to you. Read all of them. Study the ways that apply to you. That will help you bring your attention to how you stop yourself from experiencing what you are feeling.

Also study the ways that you think do not apply to you. This will help you recognize how others avoid experiencing their emotions. Once you see the emotional dynamics of another person, and how he or she attempts to avoid them, you will be able to apply that same objective perspective to yourself. You may also be surprised to discover that some of the ways of avoiding emotions that you thought did not apply to you actually do apply to you.

Psychologists call ways of avoiding emotions defense mechanisms, or forms of denial. You do not have to spend years exploring your defense mechanisms and forms of denial. You can learn to recognize them, and then use your recognition of them when they occur to direct your attention inward to the patterns of response—painful emotions—that appear in your life over and over. **Your patterns of emotional response have a life that is independent of particular external circumstances.**

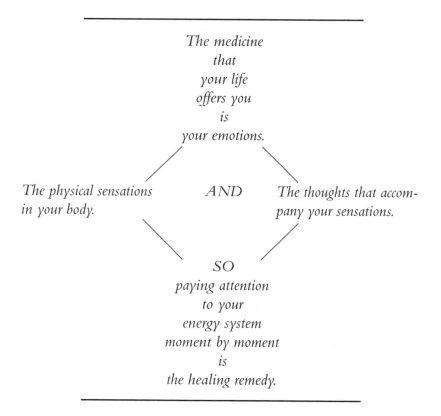

*The medicine
that
your life
offers you
is
your emotions.*

*The physical sensations
in your body.*   *AND*   *The thoughts that accompany your sensations.*

*SO
paying attention
to your
energy system
moment by moment
is
the healing remedy.*

Looking at these patterns is the first step in spiritual growth. It means cutting through all distraction in order to see clearly into the heart of the matter, which is your spiritual development. The circumstances that trigger your painful emotions are endless. **You will continue to encounter circumstances that trigger painful emotions until you look beyond them to the interior dynamics that create your emotional pain.**

When you do that, you embark upon the journey that you were born to take.

Anger

ANGER IS AN ICEBERG PHENOMENON. It is the apex of a larger structure, all of which is invisible except the very top. Anger is the snow on the summit of an otherwise bare mountain. It is the view of the mountain that you would have if your eyes allowed you to see only snow, but no summit can exist without foothills, slopes, ravines, and ridges. There can be no summit without a mountain.

In the same way, there is no such thing as anger without an immense emotional substructure. Anger is the peak protruding above the clouds. **Beneath every experience of anger is a**

"Anger is the peak protruding above the clouds."

huge body of emotional experience. Without a clear view of that huge substructure, anger cannot be appreciated any more than a mountain can be appreciated by looking at a picture of the summit from the summit. From that perspective, the summit of the greatest mountain appears to be a small pile of rocks.

Anger lashes out at a target. That target is another person, group of people, or the Universe. Anger is righteous and self-important. Anger does not listen to, respect, or care about others. It makes others wrong, to blame, inferior, or inadequate. It cares only about itself. Anger wants what it wants, when it wants it, on the terms that it wants it. It assumes the roles of judge, jury, and executioner. There is no appeal.

Discovering anger in yourself, or experiencing it in yourself again, is like finding ancient pottery in the desert, or the tops of temples that were built millennia ago and are now buried beneath the surface of the sand. This is an archaeologist's greatest aspiration. It causes boundless excitement because where there is evidence of intelligence on the surface, there is sure to be much more below the surface.

That is when an archaeological excavation begins. It continues, layer after layer, downward, uncovering new discoveries large and small as it progresses. Every shovel of earth is screened and examined with great care. Every object or fragment is noted, cataloged, and put into a special place. The deeper the excavation, the more is unearthed. Sometimes villages lie beneath cities, and sometimes cities lie beneath cities.

The dig continues until the very bottom of the richness is brought into the light of the sun. Only then is a larger and fuller picture visible—far more than could have been guessed from the initial discovery of pottery on the desert floor, or the tops of ruined temples exposed by blowing sand or eroding soil.

Anger is the pottery on the desert floor. It is the trace of a buried building. It points to much greater discoveries waiting to be revealed. **Anger is a minor discovery compared with the larger treasures that lie beneath it, waiting to be unearthed.**

Most individuals who become angry frequently think that they are familiar with their emotions because of their outbursts. They are not. They do not know what they are feeling, beyond the rage that roars through them like a storm, devastating all in its path until it exhausts itself and only damage remains. **Angry outbursts are painful experiences, but they are not emotional explorations.** Each outburst of anger is a barrier to the exploration of emotions. It is a fortress from which an individual who has no power does his or her best to face a frightening world.

Some animals snarl, hiss, or growl when threatened by a larger animal. They cannot defend themselves, so they puff up, raise fur on their backs, and show teeth. Anger serves the same purpose in humans. An individual who is angry is frightened. Only a frightened individual attacks.

All hostility originates in fear. Fear is the birthplace of every impulse that is not loving. A loving individual is fearless. An angry, jealous, vengeful, depressed, or avaricious person is filled with fear. The difference between being fearless and being fearful is the difference between a life of fulfillment and a life of dissatisfaction. It is the chasm between meaning and purpose on one hand, and despair and emptiness on the other.

Love is fearless. It does not threaten any form of Life. Love is a friend to all. It naturally nourishes, supports, and cares for others. It does not fight fear any more than the sun fights darkness. It does not know fear. Where one is, the other cannot be.

Anger prevents love and isolates the one who is angry. It is an attempt, often successful, to push away what is most longed for—companionship and understanding. It is a denial of the humanness of others, as well as a denial of your own humanness. **Anger is the agony of believing that you are not capable of being understood, and that you are not worthy of being understood.** It is a wall that separates you from others as effectively as if it were concrete, thick, and very high. There is no way through it, under it, or over it.

The connection between their anger and their fear is not one that most people make. Anger seems to generate courage beyond what is normally available. That happens when anger becomes so compulsive that it results in violence. **An angry individual appears not to be frightened at all. Actually, he or she is terrified.** It is not courage that launches the attack, but uncontrollable terror, as when a small animal, cornered and defenseless, hisses, snarls, and then attacks.

Between terror and anger lies another experience—pain. In other words, **beneath anger lies pain, and beneath that**

*"It is a wall that separates
you from others..."*

pain lies fear. It is not possible to experience the fear without first experiencing the pain. That pain may appear to be caused by the loss of a job, the death of a child, or a diagnosis of a terminal illness. The pain of these things is intense, and the experience of it is very much like feeling a white-hot piece of metal. That is why it is easier to become angry than to touch the pain. This is what most people do, but the pain does not go away when you become angry. It gets buried.

ARCHAEOLOGICAL DIG

Think of the last time you can remember getting angry. Remember the circumstances—who and what you were angry at. Take a moment to go back to this time. Remember how you were feeling. What physical sensations were you having? Where in your energy system did you feel these sensations? What thoughts were you having or expressing? Open yourself to digging deeper, to feeling what was under your anger. Give yourself permission to feel the pain hidden underneath the anger.

This is a practice you can do again and again. When you feel anger, gently allow yourself to go deeper—to dig beneath the anger.

The more the pain is denied, the greater and more frequent is the anger that covers it. **An individual who is continually angry is in continual pain.** Anger is doubly painful. The experience of anger is painful, and the pain beneath the anger is yet more intense. It erupts unexpectedly, takes control of any circumstance, and produces consequences that are also painful.

Until you have the courage to face and experience the pain that lies beneath your anger, you will continue to become angry. Your anger is away of resisting the experience of your pain. Anger is not resistance to a particular circumstance. It is resistance to the world not being the way you want it to be. Anger is pure frustration at not being able to arrange your life and others as you would like. Rage is never against an individual, an organization, a community, or any other target, no matter how much it seems to be.

ANGER IS MY RESISTANCE

Say this sentence a few times to yourself:

"I open myself to the possibility that my anger is my resistance to experiencing my pain, and my resistance to the world not being the way I want it to be."

If it feels appropriate, practice saying this sentence every time you become angry.

Rage is an excruciating experience of powerlessness. Striking out in rage is an act of powerlessness. Obtaining revenge and proving guilt are expressions of despair and helplessness. Like the small animal that attacks the larger animal, you have given up hope. There is nothing else left to do—except experience what you are feeling. Acting on anger, rage, and vengefulness are your last resorts.

They never work. The world continues to be other than you want it to be, and the pain of that does not diminish. Instead, your anger increases. You think you are consumed by an emotion, by uncontrollable anger. On the contrary, you are diverting all of your energy into avoiding your emotions and that diversion, or resistance, is the experience of anger.

Your anger is a clear, unmistakable signal that you are in pain. The Universe is directing your attention to an inner dynamic that needs to be examined. The inner dynamic is not your anger; it is the cause of your anger. That is your pain. Challenging your anger begins the process of healing what causes it. When you set the intention, for example, not to speak or act in anger no matter how angry you become, when you look for new ways to speak and act when you feel angry, you invoke the assistance of the Universe and assistance comes to you.

That assistance will take you where you need go in order to release your anger: That is to your pain—the fundamental pain of the world not being the way that you want your world to be; the pain of insisting that the wants of your personality are more important than the needs of your soul. The circumstances of your life always reflect the needs of your soul.

---

*If your dig is
deep enough
you will discover the
SOURCE
of your
pain:
The world not being the way you want it to be.
Making the wants of your personality more important than the
needs of your soul.*

There is no exception to this rule, no maybe or if. The power and beauty of a life in the Earth school is the continual encounter with precisely what your soul desires you to encounter. When you resist that, you resist the purpose of your life. You resist the beneficent Universe. You resist your nonphysical guidance and assistance. That resistance is your pain.

You continually encounter
what your
soul
wants you to encounter.
When you resist
your encounters
you resist
1. The purpose of your life.
2. The beneficence of the Universe.
3. Nonphysical assistance.
AND
That resistance
is
your
pain.

When you begin to open yourself to the experience of your pain—to the reality that the child you loved so dearly is dead, that the job you depended on is gone, that the partner you loved has left, that you have been abused and your abuser feels no remorse—you begin to move beneath the surface of your anger. You begin to transform your life. You become less rigid and less righteous. You also become more vulnerable and accepting of others and their pain. You begin to melt into the tenderness of the Universe. Before you can do that, you must breach the defenses you have created to keep you from your emotions.

This is what challenging your anger accomplishes.

When you challenge your anger, you set into motion a process larger than you can see in that moment. As you continue again and again to challenge your anger, you begin to pull your anger out by the roots. First comes the pain that your anger has covered for so long. Then comes the fear that lies beneath the pain—the terror of realizing that you cannot control all that you feel is essential to your safety and well-being. Your life is a journey into vulnerability, and you do not trust that journey. The consequence of that mistrust is terrifying.

Anger to pain to fear—those are the first steps of the process that leads to the core cause of them all. **The core cause of anger is lack of self-worth.** It is the experience of powerlessness. Powerlessness is seeing yourself as valueless, as not being able to imagine that you make a difference to anyone or anything. It is feeling that you are ignored by the Universe. It is not appreciating your importance in the larger picture of your life and the lives of others. It is ignorance of your power, beauty, nobility, and worth and denial of your responsibility for the consequences that you create.

When you feel worthless, you are terrified by your life, and when you are terrified by your life, you are continually in the pain of trying to shape your life as you think it needs to be. When that pain is acute, you cover it with anger. You strike out at friends and perceived adversaries. You mistake kindness for weakness. You cannot imagine that others care for you because you do not care for yourself. You imprison yourself in a cell that you have created. You blame everyone else for being there.

This is the archaeology of anger. It is the mountain revealed. This is the full view of the summit, the foothills, and everything in between, the majestic picture of your own complex construction and the enormity of it. It is also the perception of the compassion and wisdom of the Universe. **The Universe provides you with opportunities, again and again, without cessation, to move into the fullness of your power—into the unobstructed perception of your worth, value, and responsibilities.**

When you reach the bottom of your excavation—the final layer of lack of self-value—your anger reconfigures itself. It no longer seeks others to blame. It does not judge. Your anger becomes a positive force in your life that strives to unify rather than divide. It respects all while passionately pursuing constructive change. This is the anger that moves you to bring an end to suffering, to brutality, and to lack of reverence without adding to them. It does not separate you from love. Your love of the Earth, not your judgment of other people, makes you a proponent of the Earth. Your love of Life, not your judgment of other people, makes you an advocate of the oppressed. You do not

"This is the archaeology of anger."

seek to oppress the oppressor. You do not judge those who judge. You do not hate those who hate.

You become a light that illuminates the darkness, rather than a voice that condemns it. You bring change where no change was possible. You provide what is missing. Your anger guides you into ever more effective ways of understanding, communicating, and caring. You become a gift to yourself and others. You step into your role as a soul on the Earth, awake and aware, joyful and grateful, powerful and creative, compassionate and caring.

Workaholism

ETACHMENT IS THE DIFFERENCE between emotional involvement and emotional awareness. **Detachment allows you to see your emotions as they form, develop, intensify, and change.** Without detachment you see only the peaks in intensity. Detachment is like sonar, allowing you to see beneath the surface, on the surface, and above it at the same time.

Without detachment, you are like the *Titanic* steaming through icebergs. From the lookout's perspective, an iceberg is a piece of ice floating on the water. If the *Titanic* had had sonar aboard, the operator would have seen each iceberg for what it really was—a submerged mountain of ice. Each iceberg is the

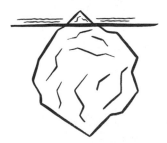

"*Detachment allows you to see beneath the surface.*"

summit of a mountain, a small part of a huge whole. Hitting an iceberg is dangerous because the iceberg is much, much larger than it appears to be.

When you move through your life without detachment, you see only the summits of your emotions. Where they come from, their roots, and the enormity of them are invisible to you. Occasionally, and sometimes frequently, you hit icebergs—you become angry, sad, jealous, vengeful, happy, or frightened. If you had an emotional sonar, you would see that each of these experiences is the summit of a much larger dynamic. Emotional awareness is the ability to see the larger dynamic. Emotional involvement tells you only that you have hit an iceberg.

Most people go through their lives from one iceberg strike to another—from anger to happiness to jealousy to fear to vengefulness, back and forth and back again. They do not know where these icebergs—sudden, forceful, and often destructive experiences—come from. They do not have the ability to see them approaching. Like the *Titanic,* they steam full ahead, looking through the fog and hoping for the best. Sometimes they recover quickly from a collision with an iceberg—from an eruption of anger, despair, jealousy, fear, or vengefulness—and sometimes the collision creates so much damage that it takes a long time to repair.

Workaholism is one way of steaming full speed ahead without even posting a lookout, much less having sonar. **Workaholism is a flight from emotions.** It is a drug that is as effective as the most powerful anesthetic. Like all drugs, it cannot mask pain indefinitely. A patient using an anesthetic must take it regularly or it wears off, and the pain returns. Even if he takes the drug every hour, sooner or later it loses its effectiveness. Then larger and larger doses are required to obtain the same results. Eventually, even large doses cannot mask the pain.

Workaholism is magnetically attractive because it prevents the experience of any emotions. A workaholic moves from one project to another, and often from one job or career to another, with the same obsessiveness. Particular projects have no inherent value. The projects change, but his workaholism does not. He is as compulsive in one project as in every other, because he is using his work to avoid feeling. He works long hours—not to finish his report on time but to anesthetize himself. The more he works, the more he needs to work. He is always only a few steps ahead of his feelings, and his feelings are painful.

The more he works, the more he must work. His fatigue becomes exhaustion, yet he cannot stop. Like a heroin addict, each fix is less effective, even though it is larger than the last and the intervals between fixes are shorter. He goes to bed late and arises early and tired to begin again. The heroin and the work serve the same function, and are addictive for the same reason—they provide temporary relief from pain. This is the profile of the obsessive high achiever.

A workaholic does not want sonar. She does not even want to be on the deck, much less looking for icebergs. She wants to live in a world without icebergs, even though they surround her. Her flight into work—raising children, teaching school, or long hours at the office—are her way of staying far below, in the darkness of the hold, pretending she is safe, and using her backlog of homework, children's needs, or always urgent requirements of her career to assure herself that she is.

DO I OR DON'T I?

If you have a suspicion that what you are doing is compulsive, ask yourself:

- "Are my projects more important than the people involved?"

- "Am I frequently impatient when I am interrupted?"

- "Do I get overwhelmed emotionally by things I don't see coming?"

- "Do I never have enough time for all that I do?"

If your answer to any of these was yes, ask yourself:

- "Do I feel the same urgency with every job, project, or activity?"

- "Do I feel I need to work all the time?"

- "Am I fatigued but can't stop?"

- "Is my work more important than my family, friends, and the promises I make to others?"

- "Am I fixated on accomplishing things?"

- "Are my activities covering up my feelings/pain?"

When the collision comes she is inundated because she is below the waterline, and unaware of what has happened. Into her fantasies crashes a waterfall of dark, icy water that cannot be stopped. Her smoothly flowing life dissolves into a depression, her frustration with a co-worker erupts into fury, or she finds herself fixated on a new dress, car, house, or partner.

Emotions come as explosions, tidal waves, or unending swamps. Where there was nothing, suddenly there is an insurmountable challenge—to forgive, to allow another to be as he or she is, or to get up in the morning. These experiences do not materialize instantaneously, but are parts of complex processes with deep roots. An eruption of emotion may appear to be caused by a particular event or circumstance—such as failing a course, a rude remark, an unmet expectation, or the death of a friend—but that is only the view from the deck which allows only a glimpse of the summit of a submerged mountain. The view with sonar reveals something quite different: the whole mountain.

Detachment is your sonar. It allows you to navigate appropriately by showing you the underwater terrain so that you know when you are approaching an iceberg and how big it is. The iceberg does not surprise you. You do not need to divert all your energy into frantically trying to avoid a collision at the last moment. You do not even pay that much attention to the tip of the iceberg, or to the circumstances surrounding its appearance on the water. You are watching the mountain.

Workaholism is the exploitation of people and circumstances in order to avoid pain. It is a narrow focus that precludes a larger landscape. It is the equivalent of putting on blinders so that all you see is the project, or need, in front of you. Your world becomes very small. You do not see others or what they are feeling, except when they affect what you are doing. You do not hear others, or listen to what they are saying, except when what they say affects you. Friends, promises, and priorities all disappear into the self-satisfying obsessive fixation on your job, career, or remodeling project.

You become irritable when others intrude in your narrow world. You are impatient with those who cannot see the importance of what you are doing. Even if what you are doing has significance to others, you do it for yourself. Your agenda is to occupy your attention. You cannot experience what you are feeling, and your awareness is fixated on accomplishment. The only emotion that you experience is the temporary satisfaction that comes with completing a project, but that is quickly replaced by the need to accomplish something else.

Workaholism is the equivalent of burying yourself in the hold of a ship, working on a trivial activity in the dark, when you are the captain. The ship is your life, and your place is on the bridge. When the captain is sweeping a remote corner below decks, her ship is bound to strike icebergs. **When you indulge in workaholism, you put strangers in charge of your life while you focus your attention on insignificant projects.** Even if your project is to create an empire, it is insignificant compared to the creation of a meaningful, aware, compassionate and fulfilling journey through the Earth school.

"you put strangers in charge
of your life while you focus your
attention on insignificant projects."

The strangers are the emotions you bury under your superficial activities. They do not disappear because you refuse to look at them or even acknowledge them. They continue to course through you, moment by moment, influencing or determining what you think, say, and do.

Emotional awareness allows you to see these powerful currents of energy clearly, feel them fully, and learn from them. **Emotional awareness allows you to walk on the Earth awake instead of in a self-imposed trance.** It is sailing with your sonar turned on instead of trying to see icebergs in the dark.

Emotional awareness is more than feeling anger when you are angry. Anger is the iceberg. Running into icebergs is emotional involvement. Your ship strikes something that cannot be ignored, and you suddenly are enraged, withdrawn, or seething with resentment. Beneath the surface of the water lies a mountain of pain.

Every collision with an iceberg—the sudden appearance of anger, jealousy, despair, vengefulness, feelings of inferiority or superiority—is a signal that you are in contact with a mountain of pain. When you focus on the summit, you remain ignorant of the mountain you have struck. Until you explore the mountain, you will strike it again and again. Each time, its summit will surprise you. Anger, jealousy, vengefulness, feeling superior, feeling inferior, or sadness will erupt, seep out, or overwhelm you. The issue is not the summit. The issue is the mountain.

The first step in developing sonar is to stop what you are doing when you strike an iceberg. When you voluntarily choose not to shout, throw something, or hit something or someone, the impulse to do those things becomes very clear to you. That impulse is the mountain, and it is very painful to experience. Most people will do almost anything to avoid experiencing it. That is why they shout, strike out, and do cruel things. They are in extreme pain.

DEVELOPING SONAR

When you feel angry, stop what you are doing, what you are saying, and what you are thinking and focus your attention on what you are feeling.

This will not be easy, but it is worth your effort. When you are in the grip of a powerful emotion such as anger, and you stop speaking and acting and start feeling, you channel the full force of that energy into your consciousness.

Choosing not to act on an angry impulse and to feel the pain that lies beneath it instead is very courageous. Even risking your life driving race cars or jumping out of airplanes does not require much courage compared to facing the pain beneath your anger. Most people do all the things that we usually think of as brave in order to avoid facing the pain that they feel.

Anger is an anesthetic. It hurts, but it is less painful than what causes it. Anger is the path of least resistance. It allows you to focus on the collision instead of learning about the mountain. **Anger is a flight from feelings, like workaholism. That is why they go together.**

Workaholism is focus on activities in order to avoid feeling. When the pain that a workaholic is trying not to feel becomes so intense that he can no longer ignore it—no matter how deeply he buries himself in work—his anger erupts. He has struck an iceberg. The life of a workaholic is a chronicle of one collision with an iceberg after another—uncontrollable outbursts of anger, deep descents into depression, days of compulsive activity, fixations on things, and obsessions with people. The duration between collisions may be days, weeks, or months, but the collisions always come.

The mountain does not go away, no matter how many times the summit is encountered, studied, or discussed in therapy. The summit does not disappear when the mountain is in view, either, but it no longer comes as a surprise. When you explore a mountain, you explore the summit, also. It is no longer a stand-alone experience.

When a mountain becomes fully visible, everything about it from the base to the summit can be studied and appreciated. You begin this process by intending to become aware of what you are feeling the next time you become angry instead of speaking angrily or acting in anger—before striking out in rage or withdrawing in fury. The more you do this, the more you become able to explore what you are feeling. The more you explore, the more of the mountain becomes visible.

Only you can see your mountain, and only you can explore it. As you become familiar with its ravines, pinnacles, chutes, and faces, you begin to appreciate it. The summit becomes part of a much larger whole. The more familiar you are with the whole, the less you are surprised by its parts. When you are familiar with the entire mountain, none of its parts surprise you.

That is when collisions with icebergs cease. You no longer become uncontrollably angry, jealous, depressed, or vengeful. You no longer find yourself feeling superior or inferior. You focus instead on exploring your feelings—including the pain that you are feeling. That pain increases and decreases as you explore the mountain. Even when the pain is intense, you are more interested in exploring it than avoiding it. Exploding in anger is no longer attractive to you. It detracts you from your exploration.

So does mindless work. You still function, but you are aware of what you are feeling as you do. You go to the office, school, or the laundry room, but your activities no longer mask what you feel. The captain takes his place on the bridge. The sonar operates. The ship no longer sails blindly over a magnificent mountainous terrain. All is present and visible.

Workaholism is a deep sleep. It is a self-induced trance that temporarily keeps painful emotions away from awareness. It is a flawed strategy that prevents you from utilizing the energy of your extremely powerful emotional dynamics. It is self-hypnosis that prevents you from stepping into the power and purpose of your life.

It is the painful slumber that keeps you from the eternal present moment.

Pass-through Effect

EMOTIONAL AWARENESS REQUIRES ATTENTION. **Emotional awareness is focusing on the experience of an emotion.** It is one thing to have an emotion while your attention is on something else. It is another, very different, thing to have an emotion while your attention is on the emotion.

Not focusing on an emotion while you are experiencing it is like being at a lecture and hearing the speaker but not listening to what he has to say, or sitting in front of a television while programs come and go, but not paying attention to any of them. Afterwards, you remember that the television was on. You remember that different programs came and went, but you cannot describe any of them, even if they amused you or frightened you at the time. You remember watching the television and being frightened or amused, but no more.

If you were studying television programming, you would remember exactly what programs aired, and in what order. You would think about why one program was scheduled at one time, and another one later. You would notice differences between evening, afternoon, and morning programming. You would notice how different directors utilize actors, order scenes, and choose music. You would appreciate action programs and romance programs. You would see similarities and differences between news programs on different stations. You would even notice how different colors appear on different television sets, and compare different sounds on different sets.

Emotional awareness is studying each program, director, actor, scene, and piece of music. It is listening carefully to the sounds and watching the colors intently. Emotional awareness is much more than being aware that you are having an emotion. It is being interested in each emotion, and comparing each emotion with other emotions, and with other experiences of the same emotion. **Emotional awareness is continuously studying the changing array of emotions within you,** as though you were preparing yourself for a career as a Master of Emotional Dynamics.

Becoming a Master of Emotional Dynamics requires you to develop the discipline to look inward, observe carefully, and apply your analytical and intellectual skills to what you see. Some people cry, laugh, become exhilarated, grieve easily and frequently. They are like corks bouncing on the waves of a turbulent ocean. They cannot find their bearings on a sea of emotions, and they are overwhelmed.

These people are no closer to becoming Masters of Emotional Dynamics than individuals who enclose themselves in a fortress of thoughts. Being tossed helplessly from emotion to emotion and isolating oneself in mathematical theorems are both ways of avoiding painful emotions. There are numerous ways to avoid painful emotions. None of them is effective indefinitely, and all of them delay addressing the underlying causes of painful emotions.

Throwing yourself into activities—such as reading, writing,

creating businesses, cooking, and shopping—are easily recognizable ways of avoiding painful emotions. Soaring into exhilaration and plummeting into despair are not so easily recognizable, but they, also, are ways to avoid emotions that are painful to confront. In other words, individuals who appear to be conversant with their emotions are not necessarily emotionally aware.

Reading a foreign language phonetically gives the appearance of knowing the language. In fact, the reader may not know even a word of the language. He knows only which sound to make when he see certain combinations of letters. People who speak the language understand his sounds, but he does not. His literacy is an illusion.

EMOTIONAL LITERACY

When you are swept away by feelings such as anger, jealousy, sadness, or depression, stop what you are doing and move your attention to the area of your heart. Allow yourself to feel whatever you are feeling. Notice where in your energy system you are feeling physical sensations or discomfort. Open to the possibility that this experience is an opportunity to learn about your emotions and to learn more about yourself.

Individuals who are emotional frequently do not know the meaning of what they feel. They do not know what lies behind their experiences any more than a person who is reading a language phonetically knows the meaning of his sounds. She shouts when she feels a particular inner experience, which she calls an emotion. She withdraws moodily when she feels another. Yet another causes her to cry, and another to laugh.

Eventually, she observes that her shouting, crying, laughing, and moods affect others. When she feels the impulse to cry, shout, laugh, or withdraw, she knows the consequences that these behaviors create, and she begins to use them to create those consequences. She does not think in terms of manipulating other people. She feels an experience, which she calls an emotion, expresses it, and creates a consequence. This is the same as observing which sounds, when reading a language phonetically, create which consequences and using those sounds to create desired results.

In the realm of language, combinations of letters become known, the sounds that express them become learned, and the consequences of those sounds are remembered. All of this can happen without knowledge of the language. She has learned to speak a pseudo-language, yet she is illiterate.

An individual who uses her emotions this way is emotionally illiterate. She speaks a language that she does not understand in order to create consequences that she desires.

Literacy requires dedication and work. It is not easy to learn a language, and especially to learn it well enough to express yourself eloquently. Learning an alphabet and the meaning of words is the beginning. Combining letters into words and words into sentences is part of the process, and so are expressing thoughts with sentences and combining sentences into paragraphs and paragraphs into larger contexts.

Mastering grammar, spelling, syntax, and style are yet other parts. At last comes living the language—thinking in the language, understanding in the language, and knowing yourself in the language. All of this is very different from learning a language phonetically. When you master a language, it becomes your instrument of expression. You know the grammar and you have a large vocabulary. You can describe everything. You do more than use your language to get what you want. You can express what you feel and you can communicate delicate feelings and complex thoughts.

The difference between an individual who can manipulate others through phonetics that she has learned and an individual who has mastered a language is the same as the difference between someone who knows how to grunt and someone who is an accomplished singer. Someone who is moved emotionally but does not take the time to explore his emotions, to become knowledgeable about them, and to recognize them and the contexts in which they arise knows how to grunt. Grunting is not a deep experience. Mere awareness of emotions is surface deep, even if the emotions appear to be, or feel, very deep. Emotional experiences do not penetrate. They pass through the one who feels them without leaving traces behind. He or she does not change.

This is the pass-through effect. Emotions are frequently experienced and used to manipulate others, but the one who experiences the emotions remains the same. She appears to others as emotional—sometimes very emotional—but she is as challenged to become emotionally aware as the individual who isolates himself in his intellect. People who are compulsively intellectual do not know what they are feeling. They frequently think they do not have emotions. They know that they are not emotionally aware. They must look for their emotions, and even when they experience intensities of anger or fear, they believe they are emotionless between these experiences.

Emotionally oriented people think that they know what they are feeling because they are often emotional. They consider themselves emotional, but they are frightened of feeling their emotions. Emotions pass through them in the same way liquid passes through a hollow reed. The emotion that passes through her in the form of emotional expressions are as effective in controlling others as carefully calculated manipulations. She does not change in response to the emotions that she feels. Instead, she uses her emotions to change the behavior of others.

ARE YOU EMOTIONAL?

Do you consider yourself an emotional person? Do you:

1. **Feel it is your right to express what you are feeling?**

2. **Often feel overwhelmed by your emotions?**

Do others say that you are:

Too emotional

So emotional

Too sensitive

So sensitive

If so, try this practice.

Every time you feel emotional, for instance angry, sad, or jealous, stop to feel what you are feeling. Ask yourself, "What physical sensations am I having in my body, and where in my energy system am I feeling these sensations?"

Let yourself feel what you are feeling, such as anger, sadness, or jealousy for at least one minute before you act the way you usually do when you feel this way.

Then lengthen the time that you let yourself feel before you act in your habitual way.

Passed-through emotions are like ripples on the surface of the ocean. They are not the same as currents that run deeper. Even when the surface of the ocean is turbulent and waves tower above ships, conditions a few hundred feet below are very different. The ocean is thousands of feet deep.

The pass-through effect allows individuals who frequently experience emotions to utilize what they feel in the same way sailors use the surface conditions of an ocean to get them where they want to go. Individuals who use the pass-through effect are sailors who know little or nothing about the ocean on which they sail.

Developing emotional awareness is a class in oceanography. It is a deep-sea exploration that reveals different currents at different levels. It measures water temperature at different depths, and clarity of the water. It studies the sea creatures that inhabit different depths, currents, and water conditions. It tracks the terrain of the ocean floor, and maps its valleys, ridges, peaks, and canyons.

Depression, for example, is a surface emotional phenomenon, even though it is a very painful experience. It is a complex combination of numerous lines of force intersecting in the experience of being depressed. Experiences from infancy, childhood, and other lifetimes each contribute. The influences of parents, siblings, and peers affect perception and understanding. The collective consciousness of millions of individuals who are similarly oriented reinforce and expand painful sensations and thoughts. Complex emotional currents combine to give expression to a unique experience of powerlessness.

The depths of this experience cannot be plumbed without emotional awareness. **The experience of depression with-**

out the perspective that allows it to be utilized as an instrument of spiritual growth is the same as drifting on an ocean of pain in a vessel that is seaworthy, and not taking the time to learn how to sail it. You are tossed by waves, moved by the wind, and carried by every current.

Anger is one of those currents. It always accompanies depression. Some people feel so depressed that they do not know that they are angry, and others feel so angry that they do not know they are depressed. Feeling the symptoms of a depression without experiencing the anger beneath it, or feeling the anger beneath it without experiencing the symptoms of depression prevents a fuller appreciation of the entire emotional process.

Anger, also, is not a simple phenomenon. It is much more than chemical imbalances in the hormonal system or cerebral cortex. Each experience of anger comes from the interaction of numerous systems of energy. There are thousands, and sometimes millions, of these systems—from other lifetimes, from other energy fields, from energy fields you are crossing through, and from the evolution of the dynamic of human anger. All of these things are at work in one episode of anger. Some components in an instant of anger are thousands of years in the making. Anger is the registration in your consciousness of the interaction of these many fields, and your response to that experience affects them.

Beneath these currents flow others. Anger is triggered by the world not being the way you want it to be. A loved one dies, a business fails, a relationship collapses, or you are diagnosed with a terminal illness, and suddenly you are filled with anger. You are treated rudely, a friend is dishonest, your new car has unfixable problems, and anger roars within you. It is easier to become angry than it is to experience the pain that lies beneath anger.

Anger is the path of least resistance. It is the more traveled road. **Rage, emotional withdrawal, seething resentment, compulsive criticism, and the hunger for revenge all mask a pain so intense that it is unapproachable.** Until that pain is acknowledged, and experienced, it continues to trigger anger and depression.

THE PATH MORE TRAVELED

Each time you feel emotional—sad, angry, jealous, frightened—ask yourself, "Do I want to take the more traveled path of expressing myself immediately and doing what I usually do, whether it is shouting, withdrawing, crying, etc.?

OR

Will I take the less traveled path—to feel what I am feeling and really explore the physical sensations in my body, and where they are in my energy system?"

If you decide to take the less traveled path, say to yourself, "I allow myself to feel these emotions without expressing myself or acting in the ways I usually do."

Anger and the depression are not problems—they point to problems. Beneath the pain that lies beneath anger lies an ocean of fear. This fear is more than fear of the dark, of an animal, or of being rejected. **It is a terror of being alive—of not belonging, of being alone, and of being unable to survive. This terror is not a reaction to particular circumstances.** It is horror of living in a world for which you feel unprepared and in which you feel powerless. It is a tidal wave that cannot be out-run and cannot be survived. It is imminent destruction that cannot be avoided.

At the bottom of this entire emotional dynamic lies the origin of all of these painful experiences. That is lack of self-worth, the experience of being without value—to yourself, others, and the Universe. **Lack of self-worth is the fundamental source of all emotional pain.** It is the root of the plant. Anger and depression are flowers. Pain at the world not being the way that you want it forms the branches. Terror at being alive is the trunk. Lack of self-worth is the root.

You may have admirers, friends, and loving family. You may exceed all your goals. The lack of self-worth that underlies this complex emotional dynamic exists independently of your accomplishments or lack of accomplishments. It continually generates terror, emotional pain, anger, and depression. It cannot be uprooted by altering the external world. No amount of doing, accomplishing, praise, or admiration can touch it. No amount of love, caring companionship, or support can diminish it.

This is the experience of insecurity, unworthiness, and lack of value. It is the core experience of powerlessness. Reaching outward to fill this inner hole, or lack of self-worth, is the pursuit of external power—the ability to manipulate and control. The pursuit of external power has been the way that humankind has evolved since its origin. Now that is changing. The new evolutionary pathway of humankind is looking inward, finding the sources of its insecurities, and healing them. That is the pursuit of authentic power—the alignment of the personality with the soul.

Your emotions are signposts that point to parts of

"*Emotions are streetlights*
on a dark night that
illuminate the road."

yourself that require healing. They are streetlights on a dark night that illuminate the road. They are broadcasts, particularly created for you alone, of information required for you to grow spiritually.

Emotional awareness and spiritual growth develop together. As you become aware of everything you are feeling all of the time, you embark upon the path of spiritual growth. You cannot embark upon this path and remain ignorant of your emotions. **Ignorance of your emotions results in your being controlled by parts of yourself that are generating your emotions.**

The pass-through effect keeps you in the control of those parts.

Perfectionism

THE PERFECT LIST (continued)

When you are finished, do the same thing with each item on your Perfect list. Notice how you feel when you think about each perfect situation, thing, or person. Make a note of the physical sensations you are feeling in your body, and what energy locations they are near.

Compare what you feel when you think about perfect situations, things, and people with what you feel when you think about situations, things, and people that are not perfect.

Perfectionism is the assumption that the world is not perfect. This assumption is incorrect. Every circumstance is perfect. Pristine nature and a garbage dump are both perfect. The first is a perfect example of the plant and animal domains developing together naturally without human disturbance. The second is a perfect example of exploitation and lack of reverence. The first reveals perfectly the balance and beauty that surrounds us naturally. The second illustrates perfectly how we can disrupt that balance.

Perfectionism assumes that one choice is better than another. **All choices create perfect consequences.** Some choices create consequences that are more destructive than consequences created by other choices. Some choices create consequences that are more nurturing, but all choices create consequences that are perfect—consequences that could not have been otherwise, given the choices that created them. A choice to exploit another person cannot create a bond of respect and appreciation. It can create only violence and destruction. Yet when even violence and destruction appear, it is incorrect to say that they are not perfect consequences, given the choices that were made.

The choice that each individual makes, moment by moment, is not between a perfect world and an imperfect world, but between different perfect worlds. Which perfect world do you prefer—pristine nature or a garbage dump? Respect and appreciation or violence and destruction? The choice is yours, but your choice is never between what is perfect and what is flawed. It is between perfection and perfection.

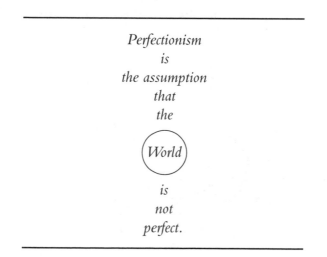

Perfectionism
is
the assumption
that
the

World

is
not
perfect.

Striving to avoid imperfection is useless. There is no such thing as imperfection. Every circumstance is perfect, given the choices that created it. You can only choose which perfect circumstances among countless ones you will create. When you judge one circumstance to be superior to another, you confuse your preferences with perfection. They are not the same.

What you prefer is not superior to what others prefer. What you create with your choices is not superior to the creations of others. When you attempt to impose your preferences on others, you do not create a world that is more perfect, you create a world of insensitive imposition. Whether you honor others or impose yourself, the consequences you create are the perfect products of your choice. When you honor others, your life fills with joy, gratitude, and appreciation. You bloom like a flower in the spring. When you impose yourself on others, your heart closes. You live in fear. Your preferences become a painful fortress, and you keep those who do not share them outside.

"You bloom like a flower
in the spring."

The pursuit of external power—the ability to manipulate and control—is insisting that the circumstances you prefer are perfect for others. It creates only violence and destruction. Honoring the preferences of others creates harmony, sharing, and cooperation. It reveres Life. That is the pur-

*"Your preferences become
a painful fortress..."*

suit of authentic power—the alignment of the personality with the soul.

Judging your circumstances to be imperfect keeps you from seeing clearly the choices that you have made—the choices that created your circumstances. In other words, it prevents you from taking responsibility for your circumstances. A lonely person who longs for a perfect world of companionship, for example, ignores the choices that created his painful isolation, choices that he himself made. He blames others for not understanding him and he blames himself for being unworthy. She rages at the Universe and she stands defiantly as a victim. She will remain that way until her pain becomes so great that, at last, she looks into her own role in the creation of her painful experiences.

When you can see clearly the relationship between the choices you have made and the circumstances around you, you will see the perfection of your circumstances. Then you will be able to change them. Until then you will regret your circumstances, be surprised by them, reject them or cling to them. You will see yourself at the mercy of a random dynamic, or a capricious universe.

PERFECTION

When you do something that you feel is not perfect—something that you would usually be upset with yourself about, such as locking the key in your car, or losing your wallet:

Stop and notice what you are feeling and where you are feeling it in your energy system.

Then say to yourself, "I am so glad that I have done this perfectly."

When someone (especially someone close to you) does something you usually judge as (definitely) not perfect:

Notice what physical sensations you are having in your body and where you feel them in your energy system. At the same time, say to yourself, "I am so glad to have this perfect person/circumstance to teach me about myself."

The dynamic that creates your circumstances is not random. You are that dynamic. You create continually and perfectly. Whether you make your choices consciously or unconsciously, you create circumstances and experience them. This dynamic is perfect. The circumstances that you create are perfect because they always reflect your choices. Every circumstance offers you an opportunity to see the relationship between it and the choices that created it, the choices you have made.

Perfection is everywhere. It is in the creation of your circumstances, in your circumstances, and in the potential for insight that your circumstances offer you. It is your life and all that is in it. It is the lives of others and all that is in them. It is the never-ending experiences that provide you, in each moment, opportunities to see the relationship between what you choose and what you experience. It is the compassion and wisdom that continually nudge you toward greater awareness and freedom.

Perfectionism is the process of ignoring what is already perfect. It is a flight from the power of the present moment, and fear of feeling it. **Perfectionism is an intellectual exercise that draws attention away from emotions and prevents the exploration of your creative power.** It is an avoidance of your responsibility. It is perpetually building sand castles before an incoming tide. Each collapse of a castle creates an urgent need to build another. Neither the castles nor the tide is important. Only the endless building is important. That is the experience of perfectionism.

When you strive for perfection, you compare different pictures of what could be instead of being present with what is. Perfectionism is an ongoing experience of the grass being greener on the other side of a fence. You are always on the less green side, striving to make your side look like the other side. Perfectionism is leaking energy to a future that does not yet exist. It takes you away from the present moment, where your power resides, and into an imaginary future. In that future, your desk is cleared of all work that needs to be done, your house or apartment is arranged as you desire, and others behave in ways that you approve.

While you are striving to make your circumstances, yourself, and others perfect, you cannot appreciate what is on your desk and what you feel when you see your desk stacked high with items that require your attention, how your house or apartment actually is and what you feel about that, how others behave toward you and how you feel about their actions. **Perfectionism is an attempt to inhabit an imaginary world in order to avoid experiencing the world in which you live.**

FRUSTRATE THE NEED

If you are a perfectionist, stop what you are doing when the urge is strong to rearrange, continue late into the night, or expand the domain that needs to be perfect, and feel what you are feeling. Your first experience will be an almost irresistible need to proceed with what you are doing. Ignoring that need will immediately create painful experiences within you. When you frustrate the need to create perfection, you will experience the pain that creates it.

If you are a workaholic, stop when the amount and urgency of what you have to do seems overwhelming, and you will experience a pain so intense that the need to recommence your work will be almost uncontrollable.

Let yourself feel it.

Experiencing the world in which you live requires your heart. You cannot grasp it with your intellect and your five senses. They provide you with only part of the picture—the part that you can see, hear, taste, touch, smell, and analyze. The whole picture requires becoming aware of all that you are feeling. Perfectionism is a mechanism that prevents this, covering painful feelings with thoughts and activities, each in pursuit of a fantasy in which those feelings do not exist.

Avoidance of painful emotions generates compulsive cleaning, organizing, and completing—at least temporarily—task lists. It fixates your attention on how your circumstances should be, and masks how you feel about the way they are. Every "ism," including perfectionism, is a compulsive need to control created by fear of painful emotions. It is the search, imposed on your circumstances, yourself, and others, for a solution to emotions that are too painful to experience.

Every impulse to create perfection is the pursuit of external power. It is looking outward in an attempt to soothe painful experiences by rearranging the external world instead of looking inward to locate the sources of your pain and heal them.

Perfectionism is an enforced rigidity that prevents the natural flow of energy and intelligence—the energy of your emotional experience and the intelligence of the Universe attempting to guide you. When you focus on your idea of perfection, you are not aware of your energy system, of how energy in your energy system is being processed, or where. Your concern is only with changing your physical circumstances.

As you pursue your ideas of perfection, more circumstances appear that need to be changed. You believe you are moving toward a goal, but the destination that beckons to you—a world in which you are caught up with your work, loved, attractive, and worthy—forever recedes before you. You cannot reach it any more than you can arrive at the horizon. You are never caught up with all that you have to do. No matter how much weight you lose, you never feel attractive. No matter how much you accomplish, you never feel competent. No matter how much you are loved, you never feel lovable.

You see yourself and others in a harsh and cruel light. Your clothing, house, activities, words, and life appear inadequate no matter how much you work, change, and improve. Perfectionism is the continual judgment of yourself and others as deficient. The more you judge, the more deficiencies you see.

Perfectionism establishes a residence in your mind and an imaginary future, but your emotions do not stop while you focus on perfection. They continue to motivate your behaviors, affect your perceptions, and change your body. Perfectionism and anxiety go together. Anxiety and ulcers, gastric distress, muscle tension, high blood pressure, and chronic fatigue go together, too.

Perfectionism is the opposite of emotional awareness. **Emotional awareness is relaxing into the present moment, even when the present moment contains painful emotions.** It is allowing everything you are feeling into your consciousness. It is observing the functioning of your energy system moment by moment. It is identifying types of thoughts with physical sensations. It is feeling what is within you as well as seeing what is around you.

Perfectionism is a perpetual flight into an illusory future that cannot be attained. It is a hunger that cannot be satisfied, a thirst that cannot be quenched, and pain that cannot be relieved. It is a persistent and painful drama that lures your attention away from what can feed you, nourish you, satisfy you, and fulfill you.

Pleasing

THE DESIRE TO PLEASE OTHER PEOPLE **is a potent way to distract yourself from what you are feeling**. While you are trying to avoid the displeasure of others, you are in extreme displeasure yourself. You are tense and ready for the worst. Your focus is on other people and what they are experiencing. You ignore your own experiences, except those of anxiety and fear.

The impulse to please other people is a powerful dynamic that is generated by fear of loss. You think that you cannot live without that which you fear losing, and so the need to gain the approval, admiration, caring, and love of other people is intense. Emotionally, it is a life-and-death matter. When other people show displeasure, it creates terror in you, which is extremely painful. It contracts the muscles, accelerates pulse and respiration, and focuses attention narrowly, among many other things. All that matters is pleasing another, or others.

If those whom you are trying to please cannot be pleased, this terror becomes more intense. The more intense it becomes, the more painful it becomes, and the greater becomes the need to please. The impulse to please is not the experience of terror or the physical pain of terror. It is a mask that covers the depth and intensity of the pain. It not only hides this pain from others, it hides it from you, also. Like anger, the need to please covers extreme pain.

Anger is rebellion against circumstances or others. It is the pursuit of external power—the ability to manipulate and control. The purpose of anger is to alter the behavior of others and, by doing so, make the one who rages feel better. The desire to please is the other side of the same dynamic. **The desire to please is an attempt to change others in order to make the one who pleases feel better.**

Anger and the need to please are both generated by fear of extremely painful emotions. They are capping experiences. They put a lid on what you feel. In neither case does the underlying pain come into awareness. In the first case, it is covered by rage. In the second instance, it is blocked from awareness by a narrow focus on what others are feeling.

Individuals who attempt to please and individuals who become angry both have authority issues. They are competitors in the pursuit of external power. The one who rages pursues it overtly, while the one who attempts to please pursues it covertly. Only the form of manipulation is different. Each keeps others at a distance. Each is intent on controlling others and each is frightened. Each is attempting to find the identical missing piece, but in different ways.

Individuals who need to please and individuals who dominate through anger and rage always find one another. They are colleagues in the Earth school who are enrolled in the same class. It may be a father who dominates and a daughter who becomes submissive. It may be a mother who rages and a son who becomes focused on avoiding her anger. The challenge for all is to develop the ability and the courage to confront the pain that lies beneath their behaviors.

When either the desire to please or the impulse to rage is frustrated—for example, when an individual remains silent in the presence of that urge—the pain beneath it emerges into consciousness. That experience is so uncomfortable that it immediately activates rage or pleasing behavior. Eventually the pain of the consequences of attempting to please others or to dominate them through anger becomes more intense than the pain that generates the pleasing and angry behaviors, and exploration of the roots of the need to please and the impulse to rage begins. If it does not, the individual dies with those patterns of behavior still in place, and another personality incarnates with the same patterns to continue the process of discovering them, and healing them at their roots.

In other words, **healing the need to please or uncontrollable anger is a sacred task.** It is part of what you were born to do, and doing it is necessary before you can give the gifts your soul desires to give, which is also part of what you were born to do. When an individual challenges his desire to please others, or to become enraged, he sets foot on the spiritual path. She begins the process that, when completed, will result in an authentically empowered personality—one in alignment with its soul.

An authentically empowered personality naturally creates harmony, cooperation, sharing, and reverence for life. You cannot create these when you are trying to please someone. **The intention to become what you think another person wants you to be disrupts harmony, even though it may temporarily reduce tension.** It prevents cooperation and sharing. You cannot express creativity, except those parts of yourself that you think will be welcomed. You cannot revere others—relate to them soul-to-soul—and so you cannot utilize the vast depth and power of your presence on the Earth, or appreciate theirs.

An individual who needs to please is constantly trying to see how others are feeling so that she will know how to be with them. She cannot take their requests and communications at face value. She tries to guess what they are really saying or requesting. That is because she, herself, does not communicate what she is feeling, thinking, or requesting. Her expressions are obscure, leaving her room to maneuver in case her communication, feelings, or thoughts arouse displeasure.

If another person is unhappy, she tries to determine how to make that person happy so that she will be more safe. If a colleague, parent, or even a child becomes upset, she becomes frightened. She feels that the smallest mistake can have terrifying consequences, that she must be careful of how she speaks and acts in order to avoid rejection, and she is constantly vigilant for displeasure.

In other words, **an individual who needs to please is always tense.** Anxiety is his constant companion. Imagine someone who is always with you, and who always brings your attention to possible disasters. He is never quiet. Wherever you go, you hear your friend speaking close to your ear. Other conversations may occur around you, but you cannot hear them. His is the only voice that you hear.

Emotional awareness requires listening to many conversations simultaneously. Energy continually leaves your energy system in different ways through each center, and each way is a conversation that occurs for your benefit. Energy may leave the location at your solar plexus (third center) in fear and doubt, for example, and cause butterflies in your stomach. That is one conversation. Energy may leave the center at your throat (fifth center) in fear and doubt and cause your voice to become raspy, or your neck and shoulders to become tight. That is another conversation. When energy leaves the center near your heart (fourth center) in fear and doubt, creating uncomfortable sensations in your chest, that is yet another conversation.

HOW PLEASING IS YOUR PLEASING?

Think of a time when you knew you were trying to please someone. Remember this occasion clearly. How were you feeling? Scan your energy system. Notice where you are feeling tension. Is it in your neck? In your shoulders? Do you have a headache? Is your chest tight? What thoughts are accompanying these sensations?

If you were able to please someone in this situation, how did that make you feel?

If you were not able to please anyone, how did that make you feel?

Next time you feel the urge to please someone, stop to feel. Do a scan of your energy system. Notice where you are feeling tightness and tension. Notice what other physical sensations you are feeling, where are you feeling them, and what thoughts you are thinking.

All these conversations are worthy of your attention. Each points to energy leaving your energy system in fear and doubt. Energy leaving your energy system in love and trust also creates physical sensations—more conversations. The conversations that your energy system generates for your benefit are always beginning, ending, and changing.

The person who focuses on pleasing others is unaware of most of them. His thoughts are on fearful possibilities. His body is tense. His awareness is filled with anxiety, tension, and a continual assessment of what is necessary to please. He is like an animal on a treadmill, running but not changing position. The faster he runs, the more quickly the treadmill turns. He worries about how he appears to others. He cannot know how others see him, so he must guess. His body, clothing, speech, and behavior are important to him for that reason. He is always aware of them and the impact he thinks they have on others.

He learns to have no opinion. When one is requested, he freezes. He will not speak for fear of rejection. He must hear the opinions of others first in order not to offend. The opinions of others, like the needs of others, are more important to him than his own. Pleasing seems natural to him because he does not see himself as worthy of the concern that he directs outward. His strategy is to focus on others so that he will be accepted by them. **One who pleases places his self-worth into the hands of others and depends completely upon their judgment— while doing his best to influence their judgment.**

She ignores herself. Because she does not take care of herself, she waits for others to take care of her. She does not feel worthy to ask for what she needs. When she does not get it, she becomes resentful. She feels that her devotion—compulsion— to care for others is not reciprocated, but when it is returned, she cannot accept it. She cannot allow others to care for her because she does not believe that they want to. Her feelings of unworthiness prevent her from believing that others could care for her, and so she suspects that those who appear to care for her have hidden agendas. She cannot accept love or caring from others because that does not fit her self-image.

WHY AM I PLEASING?

If you find yourself wanting to please, stop and allow yourself to feel what is beneath the surface.

Notice when you find yourself sensing what someone else is feeling. Ask yourself, "Am I feeling love and trust, or fear?" Stop and feel what you are feeling. Are you interested in how that person is feeling because you would feel more secure if he or she would do what you want him or her to do, or say what you want to hear?

If he fails to create the acceptance that he seeks, he feels inferior, rejected, upset, and despairing. The wind leaves his sails. He is exhausted by unsuccessful efforts. Feelings of unworthiness overwhelm him. He interprets disagreement as rejection, and inquiries as accusations of incompetence.

If he thinks about the incident later, he becomes resentful, and his resentment is deep because it is generated not only by that experience of rejection but also by the many experiences that preceded it. His continual search for signs of rejection develops into a hypersensitivity, and he frequently construes words and actions as the rejection he seeks to avoid.

Resenting and pleasing conflict. Therefore, resentment is buried while he attempts to please, but when his attempts fail, resentment emerges. If he does not feel safe enough to express it, he becomes consumed with hurt. He feels invisible and unworthy. Occasionally he feels his resentment, but expressing it is not possible.

When the pleaser does feel safe enough to express her resentment, it is with other individuals who need to please. When

DIFFERENT SIDES OF THE SAME DYNAMIC

Need to Please	Resentment/Anger

HOW THEY APPEAR TO BE DIFFERENT

Need to Please	Resentment/Anger
Submissive	Dominating
Worries how he appears to others	Does not care about others
Thinks of fearful possibilities	Feels righteous
Learns to have no opinion	Opinionated
Strives to be approved by others	Searches for signs of rejection
Manipulates through doing for others	Manipulates through anger
Buried resentment	Overt resentment
Compulsion to care for others	Pushes others away
Focused on others	Wall of separation from others
Fear of loss	Rebels against circumstances
Rages when safe enough	Pleases when frightened enough

HOW THEY ARE THE SAME

Need to Please	Resentment/Anger
Feels unworthy	Feels unworthy
Body tense	Body tense
Authority issues	Authority issues
Intention to control others	Intention to control others

DIFFERENT SIDES OF THE SAME DYNAMIC (continued)

Need to Please	Resentment/Anger
Pursues external power (covertly)	Pursues external power (overtly)
Frightened	Frightened

THE GOALS OF EACH

Avoiding painful, shameful emotions	Avoiding painful, shameful emotions

---

an individual who dominates through anger is unsuccessful, he doubts himself and feels insecure, creating a need to please. The one who pleased becomes, when she feels safe enough, one who rages. The one who rages, when he is frightened enough, becomes one who pleases.

Pleasing prevents you from experiencing your emotions because you are attempting to feel the emotions that other people are experiencing. You become lost in the attempt. You feel judged by one, disapproved by another, accepted by a third, and so on. Your own emotions are inaccessible to you because you are focused elsewhere.

Pleasing narrows your emotional experience to fear and anxiety, with moments of relief when you feel that you have succeeded. Then fear that you will not be able to continue shatters your relief. You feel that you are emotionally aware, but you are not. The pain of rejection remains. You cannot breathe freely, relax into your life, express your creativity, or appreciate yourself and others.

You cannot
please
and,
at the same time,
breathe freely,
relax into your life,
express your creativity,
and
appreciate yourself and others.

Others cannot appreciate you, either. They do not know who you are, and you do not know who you are. You define yourself in terms of what you think are their perceptions. Your thoughts, speech, and behavior constantly change because your estimate of their perceptions always changes. The pain of the rejection you seek to avoid goes unexplored, and continues to create the need to please.

Since the need to please at all times is a goal that cannot be accomplished, you ensure yourself an endless effort that continually takes you farther from your own feelings. This is the goal of pleasing—to avoid experiencing emotions that are too painful or shameful to confront. It is a technique to isolate you from your fear of losing love, a method of keeping you from your experience of unworthiness and the terror that accompanies it. It is a flight from all that the Universe seeks to bring to your attention and a defense against your own fullness, richness, and greatness.

The strategy of pleasing others does not appear as a strategy to those who use it. It appears as the only way that their lives can be. They cannot imagine other ways of being. Becoming aware of what they are doing and how they are doing it gives them a new perspective. It allows them to see the dynamic of attempting to please other individuals, or raging at them, for what it is—a particular way of experiencing themselves and others.

They can see for themselves that attempting to manipulate others by pleasing them, or raging at them, is not a path that everyone walks, nor is it the only path available to them.

It is one of many ways of avoiding emotions.

Vacating

VACATING IS DAYDREAMING, **absentmindedness, and inability to keep focused on the task at hand.** It is leaving behind one activity in order to accomplish another before the first is done—but without awareness of when you leave the first and turn your attention onto the second. Vacating is like taking one vacation after another. The work for which you are responsible does not get done because you are on holiday. A time to relax and refresh when you have worked hard, or when you need to refocus your perceptions and intentions, is appropriate and healthy. Vacating is not. It is an escape from the inner work you need to do. Whenever you approach that work, you take another holiday.

Your holidays are not always enjoyable. Sometimes you leave your work behind to worry. Sometimes you leave it behind to become frightened, angry, sad, or jealous. Often you leave it behind to think about a detail, minor unfinished business, an unrelated subject, or to remember a movie, a happy or sad time in your past, or to imagine a future that is pleasing or not.

When you vacate, the work you leave behind is the work you were born to do. That work is to become aware of all that you are feeling, to utilize your intentions to create your

experiences consciously, and to bring into your life the perceptions, values, and goals of the highest part of yourself that you
can reach for. That is your soul. Your soul is the part of you that
longs for harmony, cooperation, sharing, and reverence for Life.
It is also the part of you that is immortal.

Your soul has a long-term orientation toward your life. It is
not as interested in your new bicycle, job, girlfriend or
boyfriend as you are. It is interested in what you learn from your
experiences, including those of your new bicycle, boyfriend,
girlfriend, and all else. **Your soul is interested in how you
use your energy, what you create, and whether you move
into your highest potential.** It sees the experiences of your
life as part of a larger, richer, more complete picture than you
can see. It sees patterns of connection that bind you to everyone
whose path crosses yours, however intimately or briefly. It ap-
preciates the enormity of your life on the Earth, the scope of
your creative powers, and the extent of your responsibility for
how you use them.

Accomplishing the work that you were born to do is fulfilling, satisfying, and blissful. It completes you, moment by moment. Your days are filled with meaningful activity and your
nights are restful and healing. Insights and understanding inspire,
delight, and nurture you. Your creativity is ignited. Your words
and actions are appropriate. You know that you are worthy of
your life and you are grateful for your life. You appreciate others
and cherish the Earth.

When you keep yourself from this work, you keep yourself from experiencing all of this. You live a shallow life filled
with fears and activities that do not gratify you. You are concerned with goals that do not fulfill you. You feel empty, no

"You appreciate others..."

matter how much you accomplish. You long for meaning and purpose. Relationships do not ease this longing. Successes do not satisfy you.

Vacating is a way of keeping yourself from all that will bring meaning, purpose, and fulfillment into your life. It is a frequent, or continual, turning away from the experiences that are designed to assist you in the creation of authentic power—the alignment of your personality with your soul. You vacate your awareness of the present moment. Vacating your awareness of the present moment is the same as ignoring an important event in order to watch television without thinking about what you are doing.

The important event is your life, and your daydreams and fantasies are the television. Have you ever realized, after watching a television show, that you missed something important while you were watching? What if the television show lasted thirty years? What if it lasted fifty years? **When you vacate your awareness of the present moment, the present moment continues. It has no end and no beginning, but your time on the Earth does.**

How much are you aware of what you are intending as you

move through your days? How much do you listen to what you are saying? How much do you think about what you are doing—about whether your actions contribute to Life or not? Learning to recognize moments in which your awareness lapses and activities that you do not think about begin to fill your life is part of developing authentic power. It is a learning process that is at the heart of spiritual development. This process starts with emotional awareness.

Vacating is a pattern of indulging impulses that distract you in order to avoid what you would feel if you allowed yourself to become aware of your emotions. It is the habit of living a vacant life between moments of awareness. Sometimes the moments of awareness are more extended, and sometimes the indulgences are more frequent. The cause of your wandering attention is a fear of focusing on what the present moment is offering to you. In other words, it is a fear of what you would feel if you allowed yourself to become aware of your emotions.

Vacating is never in response to a circumstance, such as the unexpected announcement of a good television show, or your sudden recollection that you should buy a pair of socks while you are at the store. Circumstances are hooks that catch on to your fear of feeling your emotions. They do not pull you away from the present moment. Your fear does.

Being in the present moment requires awareness of your emotions, including your fears. It requires becoming aware of your energy system and how it is functioning. It is feeling the physical sensations in your body, and noticing where they occur in your energy system. It is noticing the thoughts that accompany these sensations.

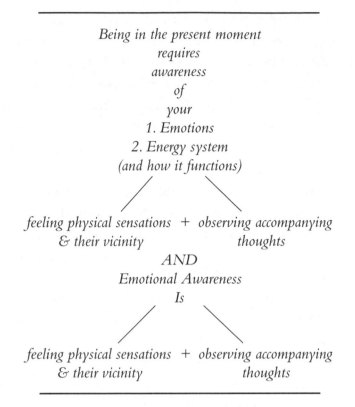

Being in the present moment
requires
awareness
of
your
1. Emotions
2. Energy system
(and how it functions)

feeling physical sensations + *observing accompanying*
& their vicinity *thoughts*
AND
Emotional Awareness
Is

feeling physical sensations + *observing accompanying*
& their vicinity *thoughts*

Without this awareness you are lost in a realm of thoughts and fantasies. Your life unfolds before you in power, depth, and meaning, but you are watching a television show in your mind. If your life ends before the show does, you will be left with the same experience of loss that you have when you realize that something important happened while you were watching a football game, or a talk show, that really did not interest you and, as a result, you missed something that did interest you.

When you reside in the present moment, your life interests you. Fleeing into your thoughts, opinions, compulsive activities, and sudden memories of details that need immediate attention takes you away from the richness and depth of your life. It is like watching television commercials in black and white, one after the other, instead of a full-color, wide-screen, surround-sound feature film with a cast of millions. You are the writer, director, and star of the movie. This is what you miss when you vacate the present moment.

Your movie is filled with events and people. Each interaction and circumstance generates emotions in you. In other words, your energy system responds differently to different people, circumstances, and events. Energy is processed differently at different centers as you encounter people and circumstances. Your body feels differently at different places and different times.

This is the movie you were born to experience, rewrite, and perfect until, at last, it is filled with meaningful scenes experienced through the emotions of a central character who cares deeply about Life. The distance between who you are now and that character who cares about other people, lives a meaningful life, and assumes responsibility for what he or she contributes to Life is the distance you have yet to travel on your spiritual path.

When you vacate your life—when you enter into periods of absentmindedness in which your attention wanders—you ignore that path. You squander the precious time you have on the Earth. There is no shame or judgment in this. There is merely opportunity that is lost in the moment. The next moment will bring you more opportunities. The opportunities the Universe provides you to rewrite the script of your life do not cease from the time that you enter the Earth school until the time you leave it. The purpose of your voluntary enrollment is to utilize these opportunities to create a personality that naturally and fully expresses the values, perceptions, and goals of its soul—harmony, cooperation, sharing, and reverence for Life.

You do not need to fear failing in this school—there is no

failure. There is only the continual choice of different ways to learn. Learning through love and trust is the most gratifying, fulfilling, and easy way to utilize the opportunities that come to you. Learning through fear and doubt is the most difficult way. It is longer and it is painful. Some people learn through fear and doubt some of the time, and through love and trust some of the time. Eventually, they see the differences between these two ways of learning and they begin to choose learning through love and trust more often.

If you are not aware of what you are feeling, you will not be able to see the differences. You will continue to fear and doubt, and your body will continue to experience painful sensations of anxiety, rage, anger, vengefulness, jealousy, self-hatred, and mistrust. These experiences are indications that you have chosen a difficult way to learn harmony, cooperation, sharing, and reverence for Life. You have, in fact, chosen to experience what your life brings when you do not strive toward these things.

When you vacate the present moment, you do not think in terms of escaping a painful emotion. You suddenly become interested in reading a letter that arrived yesterday instead of completing a task you had set for yourself. You remember to clean the bathroom and lose yourself in that for half an hour. You go to the store for a particular item and then shop for twenty minutes before you remember it.

HOW DO YOU VACATE?

At the end of each day take five minutes to go through your day. Think about when you got distracted. Remember how you were feeling before, during, and after the distraction.

Beneath each of these experiences are painful emotions that you do not want to approach, or even acknowledge. Your distractions keep you from them for only so long. Then these emotions explode into your life as anger, fear, distrust, jealousy, self-doubt, and the many ways that lack of self-worth expresses itself. The issue is your own spiritual growth. The Universe always provides you assistance. **Vacating the present moment is one way of avoiding the assistance the Universe provides you.** It is a choice to stay stuck rather than to work at changing. It is easier to turn on the television for a moment and then watch it for an hour than to face your anger, despair, and feelings of powerlessness.

When you flee from the experience of your emotions, your emotions do not stop. Your energy system continues to function. If it is creating painful emotions when you lose awareness of what you are doing, it continues. You can be sure it is creating painful emotions if your habit is to vacate the present moment. You would neither fear nor forget the present moment if it were blissful. These painful emotions create aging and physical dysfunction, and eventually they burst into your life whether you want to experience them or not. Your life is always waiting for you when you finally turn off the television, no matter how many times you turn it on or how long you watch it.

Some people spend their lives without awareness of themselves as the central character in their own movie. They do not know the experience of turning their attention inward. They focus on pleasing others, controlling others, eating, sex, achieving, or becoming invisible. They think that moments of pain, grief, and joy are the full experience of their emotions. They do not know about their energy system, how it functions, or even that it exists.

Awareness of your inner dynamics—of how your energy system is working—is the remedy for vacating. It is the grounding, nurturing substance that you crave. It is the healing that replaces the need for continual voyages into fantasy and irrelevant activities. Your energy system is a show unto itself, but this show has a purpose. **Your energy system is your personal, real-time, always-available spiritual tutor.** It provides you with information about how you are processing energy as it moves through you.

YOUR SPIRITUAL TUTOR

Take five minutes at the beginning of each day. Do a quick scan of your energy system. Pay attention to the information that your spiritual tutor (your energy system) is giving you. Practice listening to your spiritual tutor throughout the day.

That information is your emotions. **Every emotion is designed to inform you about how you are processing energy in your energy system so that you can choose to continue the same way or change.** If you continue the same way, the same painful emotions are produced. Absenting yourself from the present moment delays your discovery of what is not healthy in your life, but it does not prevent it. It is an attempted detour around what cannot be avoided.

The journey you are on is toward wholeness. Why try to find detours? Why delay your arrival at a destination that is far more satisfying, fulfilling, and enjoyable than where you are now? Why try to trade a temporary experience of drifting without awareness for a permanent experience of power and beauty?

Until you consider these questions deeply, you will continue to vacate your life.

Boredom

BOREDOM IS A FLIGHT from what is important. Like workaholism and perfectionism, it is a way of distracting yourself from inner experiences. Workaholism and perfectionism divert awareness from emotions by focusing it outward on activities. Workaholics and perfectionists distract themselves from what they are feeling by absorbing themselves in their external circumstances. They are always thinking of repairs to the house, a project that is due, an exam coming up, and so on. By focusing on activity after activity, their energy system goes unobserved.

Boredom is the failure to find an activity or circumstance interesting enough to divert your awareness from what you are feeling. It occurs when you look outward and do not find anything to engage your attention. Instead of feeling your emotions—becoming aware of the functioning of your energy system—you become bored. The experience of boredom is resistance to becoming aware of what you are feeling. It is a fertile experience because it occurs only when your search for external ways to distract yourself has failed.

Boredom is a defense against emotional awareness for workaholics and perfectionists. Workaholics and perfectionists absorb themselves in external activities in order to avoid experiencing their emotions. Eventually, those activities become exhausting. More and more remains to be accomplished or put into perfect order, but they do not have the energy to continue. That is burnout. After a vacation they begin again, and then again, until they can continue no longer. Their flight from emotions that are too painful to approach, or too shameful to acknowledge, eventually fails. Instead of turning inward to explore those emotions, they become bored.

Boredom is failure of the search for external fulfillment and refusal to look at what drove the search. **Boredom is deeprooted resistance to experiencing emotions after all efforts to distract attention from them have been ineffective.** The root of boredom is resistance to painful emotions. This is the root of workaholism and perfectionism, also. In some cases the root produces boredom first, and then an escape into workaholism or perfectionism. In other cases, the workaholism or perfectionism comes first, and then boredom.

You were not born to lose yourself in activities. Your purpose on the Earth is to give the gifts that your soul desires to give, those that create harmony, cooperation, sharing, and reverence for Life, no matter what form they take. You may raise a family, create a business, become a plumber, or go to school. Your soul will always create ways to express itself when you locate and heal the parts of yourself that obstruct its intentions.

The parts of yourself that oppose the intentions of your soul—harmony, cooperation, sharing, and reverence for Life—are the parts that are frightened, the parts that create workaholism, perfectionism, and boredom. Boredom, like perfectionism and workaholism, is a flight from your higher potential. It is fear of the transformation that wants to occur, and will occur in you, when you explore your emotions. It is your resistance to spiritual growth.

AM I AVOIDING?

List your daily activities, for example:

    Eating/snacking   Worrying

    Judging   Gardening

    Exercising

    Look at each activity one by one. Ask yourself, "How can I use this activity to become emotionally aware?"

    When you engage in one of these activities, remember to stop and do a quick scan of your energy system.

Boredom is your fuller life calling to you and your fear of hearing the call. Perfectionism, workaholism, and boredom are all ways of ignoring the present moment. Living in the present moment requires awareness of all that you are feeling—of how your energy system is functioning—moment by moment. Perfectionists and workaholics ignore the present moment by focusing on activities and circumstances. Bored individuals ignore the present moment by pushing circumstances away.

Perfectionists and workaholics lose power by absorbing themselves in activities and circumstances. They have no ability to say no to them. Bored individuals lose power by refusing to be present with their external circumstances. They have no ability to say yes to them. They push their circumstances away with the same effectiveness that workaholics and perfectionists identify with them. The result is the same—avoidance of painful emotions.

A bored individual does not value her life. She feels lost because her attempt to identify with activities and circumstances is unsuccessful. Boredom is weariness following the failure to find meaning externally, and refusal to examine the meaning of that failure—that self-worth cannot be found in external circumstances. It cannot be created by perfecting your golf swing or accomplishing goals. More imperfections and goals always appear.

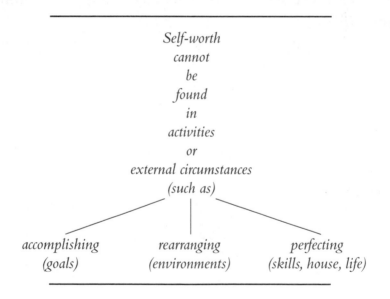

Self-worth
cannot
be
found
in
activities
or
external circumstances
(such as)

| accomplishing | rearranging | perfecting |
| (goals) | (environments) | (skills, house, life) |

Workaholics work hard because they identify their value with their efforts. While they accomplish, the pain of feeling valueless is held at a distance, out of consciousness. When they stop, it returns, driving them to accomplish again. What they accomplish is irrelevant.

Perfectionists do the same. Each has requirements that need to be satisfied. The result is continual activity. Instead of turning inward to explore the pain of feeling powerless, both workaholics and perfectionists turn outward, perfecting more and accomplishing more. Neither can stop because the pain is intense.

The bored individual cannot look at her pain, either. Lethargy and dullness replace activity. She is as controlled by her circumstances as a workaholic or a perfectionist. **Workaholics and perfectionists pour their energy into external circumstances. Bored people pour their energy into avoiding them.**

Authentic power is the alignment of your personality with your soul. It requires locating and changing the parts of your personality that are not aligned with your soul. Your soul longs for harmony, cooperation, sharing, and reverence for Life. The parts of your personality that oppose these intentions are the parts that are frightened. They are the parts that are angry, vengeful, jealous, depressed, compulsive, obsessed, and addicted.

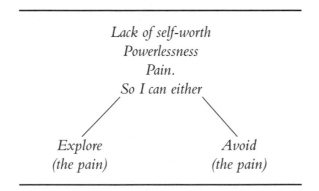

Lack of self-worth
Powerlessness
Pain.
So I can either

Explore   *Avoid*
(the pain)   *(the pain)*

The more powerful these parts are, the more an individual strives to create perfection, immerses herself in work, or is bored. Each strategy has the same goal: to avoid painful emotions. Striving to accomplish or perfect, and indulging in bored inactivity, is the same as an addict giving himself another fix. Creating more perfection, and accomplishing another goal before they become exhausted, are fixes that perfectionists and workaholics give to themselves. Boredom occurs when these fixes no longer work. It is the last defense against painful emotions—the painful experience of parts of your personality that are in opposition to the intentions of your soul.

A bored individual may find something that reignites his interest, such as a new career or a new sport. This is a return to workaholism or perfectionism. Eventually his interest fades and the struggle with boredom returns. The shift of focus from external circumstances to lack of interest and back again is actually not a change. Throughout this process, focus remains on external circumstances and activities, first in the form of attraction to them, then repulsion, and then attraction again. In every instance, the result is loss of power to external circumstances.

When an individual is obsessed with accomplishments or perfection, he loses power. External circumstances control him. When a project appears, he must complete it. When an imperfection appears, she must correct it. When you are bored with another individual, the same thing happens. You judge him or her as unworthy of your attention, and your mind goes elsewhere. Your eyes glaze and you become irritable, impatient, or sleepy. These are experiences of losing power. They occur when you assume that the person you are with is not worthy of your company. In other words, you lose power when the person you are with does not command your respect.

You also lose power when you put the person you are with above you. You assume that he could not be interested in you, and you withdraw emotionally or strive to impress. You lose power when you judge yourself, too. When you assume you are not able to learn calculus, for example, or gardening, or carpentry, your attention wanders. Boredom is a self-imposed numbness. It is a retreat into a shell, or the experience of disconnecting that results from lack of respect—of others, yourself, or your Life.

ARE YOU BORED?

Think of the last time you were talking to someone you wished you were not talking to. What did you do?

- Make an excuse to leave.

- Continue to pretend to listen.

- Use the situation as an opportunity to feel what you were feeling.

Think of a time when you went somewhere you did not want to go. What did you do?

- Become impatient, judgmental, angry (at those who made you go).

- Leave as quickly as you could.

- Use the situation as an opportunity to feel what you were feeling.

Boredom is the opposite of reverence. Reverence is appreciation of every one and everything, just because it is. It is seeing beyond the shell of appearance and into essence. Boredom prevents you from appreciating people, circumstances, and the opportunities for spiritual growth you are continually offered. It keeps you from the experience of your energy system. It prevents you from revering others, the Earth, and yourself.

Boredom also invites you to wake to the power of your life, the complexity of your experiences, and the beneficence of the Universe.

Idol Worship

I DOL WORSHIP is venerating an image. Idol worship is paying homage to, or being dominated by, an ideal. The worshiped image is perfect and powerful. It towers above mundane events and activities. The idol represents abilities not available to everyone. By gaining the favor of the idol, the worshiper obtains an easier life or relief from pain. The image holds a great deal of power to the worshiper.

The idol that most people worship, even if they are very religious and bow before statues of deities and saints daily, is not on an altar or pedestal. It is not housed in a building or kept in a garden. **The idol that most people worship every day and every night is an image inside themselves of what they think they are, or what they think they should be.** For many people, that idol is an ideal Father. For others, it is an ideal Mother. For some it is an ideal Teacher or an ideal Friend. Some people worship the idol of an ideal Soldier, others the idol of an ideal Student.

The idol is the role the worshiper thinks she must play. An idol worshiper does not think her activities are valuable except when they satisfy the idol she worships. She strives to be a role. Fulfilling that role gives her satisfaction and self-worth. If she cannot fulfill the role, she becomes depressed. She feels that she is a failure. She cannot appreciate herself apart from her ability to live her role.

The function of idol worship is to avoid living your life directly and fully. Idol worship places a screen between you and your experiences. On that screen you see yourself in a way that you believe is admirable. Your responses to circumstances are distorted by your need to fulfill your role. You do not respond directly to events. Instead, you respond in the way you think someone in your role should respond.

WHAT IDOLS DO YOU WORSHIP?

What roles do you play in your life that keep you from true connection?

Allow yourself to look closely at all the roles that you play, such as:

Businessperson

Wife

Parent

Good Person

Athlete

Etc.

Take each role one at a time and spend some time imagining yourself in your role. Notice what you are feeling. Where in your energy system are you having physical sensations and what thoughts are accompanying those sensations?

(It is okay if you do not get in touch at first with any feelings in your body. Be patient.)

If your role—the idol that you worship—is Soldier, you will respond differently than you would if your idol is Father or Friend. If your role is Mother, you will respond differently to the circumstances of your life than you would if your role were Student. **An idol worshiper ignores her inner signals and acts as she thinks she should act. Those inner signals are her emotions.**

Idol worship justifies disregarding what you feel. **If an emotion does not fit the role you think you must play— the idol you worship—you attempt to substitute an emotion you think you should feel.** If the role you play is Ideal Father, for example, you will not let yourself feel vulnerable. Your love for your family will express itself in what you provide for them. Emotions that do not fit your image of what an Ideal Father, or provider, should feel will be pushed aside. Playing the role of Ideal Father is how you push them aside.

Your emotional life is far more complex than you allow it to be. It is also far more painful than you allow yourself to experience. When you play a role—worship an idol—you remove yourself from the richness that flows through you each moment in order to identify with an image of what you believe that richness ought to be.

If you use a role to create your sense of self-worth, you are an idol worshiper. The idol you worship is the image of what you think you must be in order to be safe, admired, and valuable. Idol worship originates from lack of self-worth, or powerlessness. Instead of exploring the pain of powerlessness, you pretend it is not there as long as you follow rules that you adopt. Those rules establish how you must think, speak, and act in order to feel powerful, admired, and lovable.

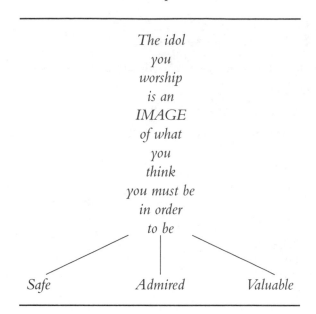

The idol
you
worship
is an
IMAGE
of what
you
think
you must be
in order
to be

Safe   *Admired*   *Valuable*

Following the rules can provide only brief experiences of safety and satisfaction. Beneath them is the fear that you will not be able to live up to your role—the idol that you worship. Your idol is not the central issue. The central issue is that you have chosen to worship an idol, and to divert your attention away from your emotions.

There are numerous ways to create and worship idols. Any image of yourself that makes you feel more handsome, beautiful, graceful, lovable, and admired is an idol. It is a picture to which you must conform in order to feel those ways.

There is no power in idol worship. Idol worship originates in fear, perpetuates fear, and expresses fear. It is a route that leads away from empowerment, not toward it. Every idol, even those that appear courageous, is a creation of fear. The Daredevil, for example, is such a role. It functions like every other idol, or role, to keep the worshiper from experiencing painful emotions.

WHY IDOLS?

While thinking about one of your roles, ask yourself the following questions:

"Why did I create this role?"

"Did I create this role to be . . ."

Beautiful

Handsome

Lovable

Admired

Appreciated

"Did I create this role to . . ."

Feel more worthy

Feel less vulnerable

Cover my fear

Ask yourself these questions again while imagining yourself in each one of your roles, one at a time. Give yourself adequate time to explore these questions.

A Daredevil creates fears to overcome in order to avoid what is truly frightening. It allows him to paint a portrait of himself that he finds admirable. The courage required to challenge the fears he chooses to confront satisfies his image of himself as brave, manly, or, for a woman, womanly. Courage is involved and goals are accomplished, but all of them divert his attention from what is terrifying, not merely frightening.

When I enlisted in the U.S. Army, I saw myself as a soldier of fortune, a formidable force in the world, not to be taken lightly. This image of myself as ruthlessly manly required that I act appropriately. I enlisted in the infantry, even though I could have avoided the military. My motivation was not love of country, although I liked that image, too. It was a deep need to prove myself worthy of admiration. In those days, I could not have brought myself to say that I wanted to be loved.

Everything I did appeared to me as an image on a big screen in which I watched myself with rapt admiration play the hero. I assumed that everyone in the theater felt the same way about me. It was much later that I realized that I was the only one watching that movie. In that movie I jumped out of airplanes, volunteered for top secret missions, carried special weapons, and was given special privileges for doing these things. I became a paratrooper, an officer, and then an officer in the Green Berets. That made me, in my opinion, the elite of the elite.

I was not looking beyond my opinion of myself. I did not have the courage to do that. I felt that my exciting life made me the envy of men, admirable to women, and valued by all. The widespread opposition to the Vietnam war did not dampen my estimation of myself as admirable and admired. I ignored what I heard and surrounded myself with those who were doing the same thing.

I was reaching for love in a convoluted way. I set up barriers against rejection by proving to myself in advance, and I thought to others, that I was worthy of acceptance whether they rejected or accepted me. I did not have the ability to feel my vulnerability. In fact, my vulnerability was driving me to do everything, including enlisting in the army. I desperately needed to demonstrate that I was not vulnerable. I attempted to become inhumanly perfect. In the process, I eliminated any possibility of genuine relations.

My relationships were limited to others who also were staring at their own movies, always playing the role of a manly or womanly, courageous, admirable, and admired hero. In retrospect, after many decades, I believe that all of my colleagues at the time were frightened. Being frightened is a part of the human experience. It lies beneath every impulse to grow spiritually—to find the roots of fear and pull them.

I was too frightened of being frightened to admit my fear. Instead, I demonstrated my courage to myself and others by physical feats of endurance and becoming more and more effective as a soldier. I thought that nothing required more courage than to be shot at by other people, and to shoot at other people who were shooting at me. All the while, I did not have the courage to look at my terror of trying and failing, of not belonging, and of reaching out and being rejected.

As a consequence, all of my relationships were shallow and mutually exploitative. I saw myself as admirable, and I expected everyone else to see me that way, too. Many people did. Yet there was no more real relationship between us than there is between an entertainer and her fans. As long as they cheered me, or I thought they did, the people around me validated my image of myself. If they did not, I found other people who did.

This is the life a Daredevil inhabits. He fears his emotions and strives to create an emotionless world of continual admiration for himself. He becomes an idol to himself as well as others. He cannot allow into his awareness emotions such as fear of rejection, lack of worthiness, or vulnerability that do not fit his picture of himself. He strives for ever more difficult or dangerous accomplishments in order to continually prove himself worthy of love.

This dynamic shapes the thoughts, words, and actions of every idol worshiper, whether the worshiped idol is Businessperson, Entertainer, Athlete, Rich Person, Poor Person, Educated Person, Farmer, Good Person, or any other role that can be adopted to create a sense of self-worth. **The idol worshiper does not have the courage to open himself or herself to love, so he or she mistakes admiration for love.** That is the most that an idol worshiper can hope for, and, in fact, it becomes the object of all her actions and thoughts. She substitutes an impersonal perception of herself as an idol for a real connection of caring and support.

WHY MY ROLE?

As you look at each role you play, put yourself in that role.

While you are imagining yourself in each role, scan your energy system. Look for what physical sensations you are having, especially if you have not noticed them before.

Ask yourself:

"Does the role I am playing give me a feeling of satisfaction and self-worth?"

"Do I appreciate myself apart from this role?"

"How do I feel about myself when I am not in this role?"

"Do I divert attention away from my emotions in order to fill the requirements of my role?"

A Daredevil sees himself as an admirably courageous person, but in fact he does not have the courage to face what he is feeling. This lack of courage is not a part of his consciousness—it is a terror that prevents him from approaching feelings of inadequacy, unworthiness, and pain of rejection. He pushes these emotions aside in an effort to do what is admirable, in his opinion, and to be accepted and valued. The more he avoids these emotions, the deeper his need to be accepted and valued becomes, and the more he creates dangerous, and seemingly admirable, challenges to overcome.

No matter how successful he is, he cannot feel the comfort he longs for. No matter how admired he is, or thinks he is, he cannot relax and enjoy his life. He is always on guard, ever playing a role, and ever terrified of being discovered. This is the experience of every idol worshiper.

Idol worshipers do not have the courage to care about people because of fear of rejection. They cannot reveal their inner torments and deepest feelings, for the same reason. Their fear of rejection prevents all connection and seals them into enclosed bubbles of their own fantasies. Others can relate only to these fantasies, not to them.

Every idol worshiper, including the Daredevil, is lonely and afraid to reach out in tenderness and openness. She is too frightened of the interactions that come with intimacy to attempt it. Her fantasy cannot survive the realities of a close and enduring relationship in which her partner does not always have the energy to support her opinion of herself, or share it. The partners she attracts have the need to share in the characteristics she feels are part of her image. They are not able to relate to her as a real and vulnerable person any more than she can relate to them or to herself in that way.

The more challenging the deeds of a Daredevil, the more frightened the Daredevil becomes of not being able to continue to earn the admiration and praise of others. He finds more and more challenging activities, each taking him further from the real care and appreciation of others that he longs for. He has no inner sense of value apart from the image he has created of himself, and so his efforts constantly go into maintaining that image. No matter what he has accomplished in the past, he must accomplish more. No matter how many times she has proven herself, she must prove herself again, ever more dramatically, convincingly, and incontestably.

She is in a contest she cannot win, because she is attempting to fill a broken container. Even if she pours new content into it every moment, it will never fill because it cannot hold what she gives it. The broken container is her image of herself. It is based entirely upon the evaluation of others, and so she can never rest from proving herself to others. At the same time, she does not realize that it is herself that she most wants to please.

This is the core issue that a Daredevil avoids with every dangerous and daring activity. It is the dark hole that has no bottom. No matter how many people admire him, his need to prove himself will continue until he comes to admire himself. His fear of rejection has a real basis—he continually rejects himself. He is looking in the wrong place for the treasure he seeks—his sense of self-worth—but he will not stop looking for it there.

Whether the worshiped idol—the role that offers a sense of value and safety—is Daredevil or Mother, Teacher or Movie Star, Hard Worker or Carefree Soul—the worshiper attempts to manipulate others with her or his activities. That is the pursuit of external power. She is on a one-way street to despair. She is always on trial, and her judge is merciless, because she is the judge, although she thinks that other people are. Her approval of herself is seldom given and never genuine. The trial becomes tiresome, but she cannot quit it because the stakes are too high.

This is far from emotional awareness. The Daredevil continually creates fears to challenge because he cannot face the deeper fears that motivate his need to find admirable, to him, challenges. He is on a treadmill, running faster and faster, and going nowhere. So is every idol worshipper.

A Daredevil is encapsulated in a self-constructed illusion of glamour. A Mother is encapsulated in a self-constructed illusion of goodness, or of a martyr. A Teacher is caught in a self-constructed illusion of knowing what needs to be taught, a Businessperson is imprisoned in the role of competitor, and so on. **No idol worshiper—player of a role—relates honestly with himself or others, and others cannot relate honestly with him.** They relate to his image, as does he. His image is the person he presents himself to be, but it is not all of who he is. It does not reach his depths or touch his richness.

It insulates her from her joys and sorrows, both of which are frightening to her. She is wrapped in the cocoon of her own creation, but she is not undergoing metamorphosis. She is fighting change. Change comes with emotional awareness. The same emotions return and return until they attract attention to themselves. That is their function. When attention is withheld or withdrawn from emotions, nothing in consciousness can change. Emotions are messengers that carry information. Spiritual growth depends upon receiving that information and using it.

An idol worshiper is committed to ignoring her emotions, and so she is committed to stagnation. The Daredevil at age twenty and the same Daredevil at age fifty are not different in their perceptions, values, or actions because there has been no spiritual growth in the intervening years. Psychological and emotional maturation have been put on hold. Relationships of substance and depth have not been allowed to occur. Only the illusion of a glamorous self persists, along with the always denied evidence to the contrary—an interior life of loneliness, emptiness, and fear.

The longer the illusion of glamour—or goodness, innocence, shrewdness, or fearlessness—is held in place, the greater is the potential shock of looking at the consequences it has created. This continues until the pain of living a shallow life without value, except for the admiration of others when admiration can be manipulated, becomes unbearable. Then the emptiness, pain, lack of self-worth, and loneliness crash into consciousness like a tidal wave.

This is the extreme scenario. It is the example of the individual who, from youth through old age, refuses to acknowledge his or her emotions and, in the process, denies herself or himself the richness his or her life offers. The illusion, whether it is of glamour, goodness, shrewdness, or any other quality, is persistent. It remains until the pain of maintaining it becomes too great to endure, and then it is finally replaced with a truly glorious life. This is the path of no inner work. It is the consequence that follows from avoiding emotions, except when they become too painful to ignore. The intensity of the pain you strive to ignore month after month, year after year, and lifetime after lifetime increases until, at last, you can ignore it no longer. That is when you change.

A glorious life is filled with companions who have open

hearts. It generates joy moment by moment. It is the continual experience of gratitude. The individual who lives a glorious life savors each moment on the Earth, and celebrates each soul—without reservation and without limitation. **A glorious life requires the courage to face the most difficult challenge that a human can face—the pain of powerlessness, of feeling unloved and unlovable—and to change.**

No idol worshiper, not even a Daredevil, has the courage to do that.

Impenetrable Optimism

I T IS NATURAL to be grateful for your life, and to look forward to each day. An individual with impenetrable optimism is not grateful for his life and does not look forward to it. He is frightened of his emotions. He cannot consider that he has created destructive consequences, that his life is not the way that he wants it to be, and that his pain is real. He lives in a fantasy. In his fantasy, all is for the best. This means, to him, that in some vague way he will accomplish the goals he desires. His greatest fear is that he will never accomplish them.

Impenetrable optimism is the story of sour grapes lived again and again in the life of an individual. A fox saw some red, ripe grapes hanging invitingly from a vine high above him. No matter how high he leaped, he could not quite reach the lowest of them. At last, in exhaustion, he decided to himself, "Those grapes are probably sour, anyway." Like the fox, an impenetrable optimist cannot face the pain of wanting the grapes very much and not being able to get them. He is not willing to acknowledge that the grapes are probably as delicious as they look, and that he still is not going to get them.

When an impenetrable optimist cannot get what she wants, she believes that she does not want it. The opposite is true. She wants it, but she cannot get it, and not getting it is a painful experience for her. She sees herself as carefree, but she is not. Her concerns are as important to her as the concerns of others are for them. The difference is that she cannot acknowledge the depths of what she feels. She would rather pretend that she is not disappointed than feel the pain of her disappointment. **An impenetrable optimist uses optimism to shield herself from painful emotions.**

This pretense masks pain of unmet expectations, pain of loss, fear of failure, and fear of rejection. It is impenetrable because she is unwilling to face the realities of her circumstances. She pretends they are not as difficult as they are. She sees herself as a victim—at the mercy of forces she cannot control—but she will not allow herself to feel the pain of being a victim. She pushes aside the powerful emotions of sorrow, despair, anger, fear, jealousy, and rage. She presents to herself and others the appearance of happy acceptance.

Eventually, the discrepancy between the pain she feels and the image she projects becomes so large that she cannot maintain the image. The shallowness of her life cannot be denied. Despair follows that is too great to be ignored, and a healing crisis begins.

An impenetrable optimist barricades herself from her emotions behind the assumption that "all is for the best." That assumption is correct. The crisis occurs because she uses that assumption to barricade herself from her emotions. Instead of experiencing them, exploring them, and learning from them, she fears and avoids them. The information that they provide goes unnoticed. At last, the emotions that she attempts to ignore confront her with a force that she cannot ignore.

Until then, she cannot begin the process of learning about her energy system, which functions with or without her awareness. It produces emotions—physical sensations—in response to each circumstance that she encounters. These emotions are accompanied by thoughts. The impenetrable optimist ignores all of this, but none of this ignores her.

The more he denies his emotions, the more powerful they become. This is for the best, but an individual with a barrier of false optimism cannot know that. "All for the best" is his defense, not his reality. It is his wall against his emotions, not his acceptance and appreciation of them.

Behind the wall is a drab world with few companions. They, also, are not able to create relationships of meaning and depth. The outside of the wall is painted in bright colors. The other side of the wall is not so attractive. It is covered with sharp edges, like broken glass. That broken glass is the shattered hopes, crushed aspirations, and painful longings that were never experienced or expressed.

Impenetrable optimism is not the same as the optimism that is born when an individual becomes aware of the compassion and wisdom of the Universe. That optimism grows like a plant in the spring, always deepening its roots

"That optimism grows like a plant in the spring..."

and gaining strength. When it flowers, "all is for the best" be-comes a description, not a motto. That kind of optimism re-quires awareness of your emotions.

Your emotions anchor you in your soul. They tell you what your soul wants you to know. They are your direct connection with your soul. Without awareness of your emotions, you drift on an ocean of experiences. Think of your emotions as a twenty-four-hour-a-day news program designed especially for you. Its information is always correct, appropriate, and timely. Anger, fear, rage, jealousy, despair, vengefulness, and every other painful emotion call your attention to where it is needed. If you do not respond, calls keep coming.

You can pretend all is for the best, but if you fear your fear, anger, jealousy, and vengefulness, you do not believe it. When you welcome your emotions as teachers, every emotion brings good news, even emotions that are painful. They tell you whether energy is leaving your energy system in fear and doubt or in love and trust. Knowing when energy leaves you in fear and doubt gives you the opportunity to change. That information is painful to receive, but without it you cannot change.

When energy leaves your energy system in fear and doubt, it can bring only pain. When energy leaves in love and trust, it creates health and gratitude. You are blissful. Comparing these experiences requires emotional awareness. Healing begins when you decide to replace the pain that results from energy leaving in fear and doubt with the bliss that results from energy leaving in love and trust.

False optimism is a blinder. It prevents you from seeing what you do not want to see, but it cannot keep you from stumbling

ARE YOU REALLY THAT CHEERFUL?

Do people say to you:

"How can you be so happy all the time?" or

"I admire how cheerful you are all of the time."

Do you feel that no matter what, you need to have a good attitude?

Is this chapter describing you, or are you strongly reacting to (disliking) it?

If your answer to any of these questions is yes, here is a practice for you: Think of a time recently when you did not get what you wanted and you said to yourself or others, "It was all for the best," but you knew deep down that you did not feel that way.

Feel yourself in that situation again. Stop. Do a scan of your energy system. Give yourself some time to feel. If you do not feel anything this time, scan your energy system whenever you do not get something that you really want, for example, affection from a friend, a hello from a stranger that you said hello to, a raise at your job.

Do this practice again. The more you do it, the more you will discover about yourself.

because of what you do not see. You run into walls and fall into chasms. Only taking off the blinders can prevent that. Wearing blinders is a temporary escape from pain. Removing them is the first step toward changing permanently what causes your painful emotions.

Entitlement

ENTITLEMENT IS THE BELIEF that you have a right to what you desire, regardless of what others desire. It is the feeling that you are not subject to rules that limit others. You see yourself above others. Their activities are unworthy of you, and boring.

Entitlement is a perception that you are fundamentally superior. When others do not share your perception, you feel unappreciated. Your feeling of entitlement does not depend upon skill or talent. You feel that you are entitled to what you desire even if you are not willing to do what is necessary to obtain it, or have not developed the abilities necessary to obtain it.

Beneath entitlement is a very different reality. An individual who feels entitled is not aware of it, and he cannot become aware of it while he sees himself as entitled. Entitlement is a mask an individual wears so that others will not know him. It keeps him from knowing himself, too. He is unaware that he is wearing a mask, or what the mask hides. The mask conceals his fears from himself. He becomes the mask, and the mask controls his perceptions, thoughts, and actions.

The mask is a way of avoiding a deep dynamic—the experience of unworthiness. She does not feel worthy of her life. Rejection terrifies her. She desperately needs to be accepted. Her entitlement is a defense, but she does not know she is defensive.

She fears people, failure, and her life. Rather than experience these fears, she feels entitled.

Entitlement is a denial. Denial does not mean refusal to admit what you know. It is blindness. It is not realizing something important about yourself. Until you learn what you deny, you cannot be free of it. If you deny a fear, you cannot free yourself of that fear until you experience it. You will create painful consequences and then be surprised by them. For example, entitlement prevents intimacy. Lack of intimacy creates isolation. Isolation creates the experience of being unappreciated. You cannot heal the pain of feeling unappreciated until you heal the need to feel entitled. They come together.

An individual who feels entitled does think that her experience is unusual. She cannot imagine being any other way, and she cannot imagine that others do not feel that way, also. Feeling entitled is like flying above the clouds and not wanting to come

"Lack of intimacy
creates isolation."

down. You believe that the sky belongs to you alone. When other fliers appear, you do not want to see them.

You consider yourself above all people and things. You look down on them. You prefer to be so high above them that you do not see them at all. You behave as if you were a king or queen. You do not enjoy the company of others except when their desires are in alignment with your own. You want the entire mountain, meadow, trail, or ocean to yourself.

Beneath entitlement is terror of ridicule and rejection. Entitlement and needfulness are directly proportional. When needfulness increases, so does the sense of entitlement. When the sense of entitlement is very strong, no meaningful interaction with others is possible. Give-and-take are not possible. You do not listen with interest or share with authenticity.

Entitlement is an illusion in which disagreement has no importance because you do not value the opinions of others. You reject others before they reject you, and you interpret your pain of isolation as a right to have solitude.

Entitlement is the feeling that you have the right to impose your will on others. It is a right that cannot be challenged. This royal solitude is barren. It is the empty sky with no other fliers. It is the pristine mountain with no other climbers. It is a life devoid of intimacy.

Entitlement requires the appearance of invulnerability. It makes asking for help and receiving it impossible. It is the feeling that no one except a peer can assist, and you have no peers. Entitlement is a self-imposed sentence of solitary confinement to a cell in which you suffer alone because no one else has the right to enter it. Your pain is beyond the comprehension of others. Your needs are beyond their ability to provide. You fear that they see you as you see them—unworthy.

The more frightened you are, the more entitled you feel yourself to be. Entitlement is like a stuffed toy that a child holds in the dark. The darker the room becomes, the more important the toy becomes to the child. Only lighting the room can remove the child's fear. Only removing the child's fear can remove its need for the toy. The toy is your feeling of entitlement. Entertaining the possibility that you are frightened is a step in turning on the light.

EXPLORING ENTITLEMENT

When you read this chapter:

1. Do you see yourself?

2. Do you feel strongly, "This is not I"?

3. Do you recognize this as the behavior of someone you know?

If you answer yes to the first two questions:

Entertain the possibility that you are frightened. Do a quick scan. Be gentle with yourself and open yourself to clearly seeing this fear. Repeat this practice each time you feel entitled.

If you answered yes to the third question:

Entertain the idea that the someone you know who is described in this chapter is frightened or he (she) would not be acting this way.

You are entitled to compassion and wisdom. You are entitled to a life of creativity, awareness, and freedom. You were meant to have colleagues of the heart. You are entitled to joy, but in cocreation with others, not in isolation. You are entitled to creativity, but in concert with others.

These experiences come naturally, as snow comes in the winter and grass grows in the spring. Entitlement is the perception of your highest potential through the filter of your fears. Entitlement is temporary protection against fear that the Universe is not big enough, abundant enough, fair enough, and gracious enough to meet your needs. It is. The needs of your soul are always provided, moment by moment.

The desires of your personality are always met when they are the same as the needs of your soul. When your personality is aligned with your soul, this entitlement can never be taken from you.

Alcohol and Drugs

ALCOHOLISM AND DRUG ADDICTION are symptoms. The cause of these symptoms is a deeper problem that must be addressed if the symptoms are to be removed permanently. If the symptoms are treated in isolation from their cause, they will reappear, and continue to reappear as long as their cause remains unchanged. **The cause of alcoholism and drug addiction is intense emotional pain.**

Less frequent dependence upon alcohol and drugs is generated the same way. The difference between addiction, frequent use, and less frequent use is one of degree. Each is an expression of the same underlying cause. Occasional use of alcohol or drugs masks discomfort too difficult to confront. It is an apparent remedy for stress, social unease, feelings of inadequacy, and fears of being judged, rejected, or humiliated. The more frequently these painful experiences occur, the more dependence upon alcohol or drugs develops.

When these painful experiences are continually present, and no effort is made to heal the causes of them, a continual dependence upon alcohol or drugs develops. This dependence may or may not be associated with physiological predispositions, or with environmental or cultural influences. It is always caused by emotional pain.

Emotional pain also has a cause. **Finding and healing the cause of emotional pain is the core of spiritual growth.** It is the work each individual in the Earth school was born to do. The causes of emotional pain are parts of the personality that are not aligned with the soul. These are parts that are in opposition to the intentions of the soul—harmony, cooperation, sharing, and reverence for Life. They have their own agendas, values, perceptions, and methods. All of them produce painful consequences and painful emotions.

Every painful emotion points the way to a part of the personality that does not share the elevated perceptions of the soul. Every experience of sorrow, despair, vengefulness, jealousy, resentment, anger, and fear is a signpost pointing toward a part of the personality that languishes in lack of trust. Finding and healing those parts of the personality creates an integrated, wholesome, joyful, aware, and responsible personality. That is the experience of authentic power.

Each diversion of attention away from a painful emotion halts a process that longs to be completed. Each painful emotion is a doorway leading to a destination you were born to attain. When you mask, obscure, or anesthetize an emotion, you turn your back on the doorway. The promise it holds for you goes unrealized, and the sources of your emotional torment remain undetected, unchallenged, and unchanged.

Beneath alcoholism and drug addiction lie layers upon layers of emotional pain. Alcoholism and drug addiction are the outermost layers. They cover emotional pain, which covers more intense emotional pain. The permanent healing of an addiction is also the permanent healing of a part of the personality that is consumed with shame and fear. Healing an addiction, including addiction to alcohol and drugs, requires an inward journey through your greatest inadequacies. Every moment of emotional pain is a place to start the journey. These potential starting places are gifts from the Universe, and messages from your soul. They tell you that an inner exploration is necessary, and that now is the time to begin it.

THE NEXT DOORWAY

Imagine yourself in the next situation where you will decide whether or not to take a drink or take a drug. Say to yourself, "Will I do what I usually do in this situation, or will I see what is behind the doorway if I do not take this drink or this drug?" Now allow yourself to feel your energy system as you contemplate this question. What physical sensations are you feeling, and where are you feeling them?

Experiment with the practice. Do it frequently. Then try it in real time, when you want to take that drink or that drug.

"I was angry," a friend wrote to Linda and me, "and I had an alcohol and drug problem. For seventeen years I went to AA and was sober. Six years ago I crashed. I became depressed and gained a lot of weight. I didn't know what to do.

"During this time, I went to a meditation retreat. When I got there I learned it was a completely silent retreat. We were instructed to not even look at anyone. I felt very strange about this, it was so different.

"At one lunchtime during the retreat, I was holding my plate of food and looking for a place to sit. Because I had gained so much weight, there were no places left on the benches in the dining room where I could fit. Since I couldn't speak or look at anyone to let them know I wanted them to move over, I tapped a woman on the shoulder at the end of a bench and she slid over for me. And again because of my weight I still could not fit into the space she opened for me. I realized if I was going to be able to sit and eat I would have to tap her again. As I tapped her again, I began to feel heat rising within me. I had to walk immediately into the kitchen. I leaned against a counter as tears began to stream down my face.

"I began to identify these feelings that were roaring through me as shame. I felt shame for how my body looked, for how much weight I had gained. Then I understood that I was feeling my deeper emotions for the first time. I was feeling the buried shame of a lifetime.

"I realized that I had done everything possible not to feel—to anesthetize myself my whole life. I felt a sudden urge to run but there was nowhere to go without taking me. During the course of the day, I let myself feel what I was feeling moment by moment without distracting myself by getting angry to cover my deeper feelings, or eating to numb myself or any of the other ways I keep myself busy doing things or thinking about things so I don't feel. It had taken a lot of anger to push the shame away. Now I feel free to feel all my emotions. I feel lighter. When I speak to people, I can tell them how a woman who was addicted to alcohol and angry made the journey from there to here."

Alcohol covered anger, anger covered shame. This is the pattern. Alcohol and drugs smother the experience of emotional pain temporarily, but, like a forest fire that spreads beneath a forest floor of pine needles, the source of emotional pain cannot be remedied so easily. It, also, spreads beneath the surface of a life, flaring in unexpected ways and at unexpected times. Until the fire is dug up, exposed in its entirety, and then extinguished, it will continue to burn. This requires work, courage, and commitment. Alcohol and drugs put out flare-ups temporarily, but the underlying fire still burns. The surface smolders and reignites. No amount of alcohol or drugs can put out the fire that is the source of the flare-ups.

Seventeen years of sobriety did not extinguish the underlying fire. It flared again into depression and obesity. Only uncovering the underlying fire can stop the entire process. Emotional awareness is the spadework required to expose the underlying fire. Shame beneath anger beneath alcoholism beneath depression and obesity was the fire that our friend fought. She extinguished one flare-up with the help of a support group for alcoholics. She might have extinguished the second flare-up with the help of diets and antidepressants. When she found the underlying fire—"the buried shame of a lifetime"—she put an end to the flare-ups that had disrupted her life—anger, depression, addiction to alcohol, and then addiction to food.

Only you can extinguish the source of your emotional pain. The emotional pain that produces more emotional pain and addiction is a calling from your soul. Alcohol and drugs are ways of ignoring the calls for an hour, a day, a month, or a lifetime, but they cannot stop the calls.

Eating

YOU ARE CONTINUALLY NOURISHED BY THE UNI-
VERSE. **When you close yourself to that nutrition, you feel the need to provide it to yourself.**
That is when food becomes magnetic. You do not have the
capability to provide yourself with the nourishment that you
crave, and so eating becomes endless. **It is not calories you
seek, but contact with your soul and with the Universe.**
That is the realm that satisfies, completes, nourishes, and sus-
tains. No amount of chocolate, chips and salsa, or macaroni and
cheese can substitute for that.

You cannot receive too much nourishment from the Universe any more than you can breathe too much air. When you
do not have enough air, you gasp. When you do not have the
nourishment of your soul and the Universe, you seek substitutes. Food is a substitute. You can eat too much food.

Eating more than you need is not necessarily a sign of
chemical imbalance, although it can cause chemical imbalances.
It is always a sign of a more fundamental imbalance that needs
correction. Until that correction is made, compulsive hunger
will continue to remind you that you have inner work to do.

**Dieting and exercise cannot reach the root of obses-
sive eating.** Eating healthy foods in appropriate amounts and

228

exercising are prerequisites for physical health. However, illnesses are symptoms of deeper dynamics that bear directly on the purpose of your life on the Earth and whether you are accomplishing it.

REASONS TO EAT

List your reasons to eat, for example:

- I deserve to eat because I . . .
- I can eat anything because I like the taste.
- I do not need my body.
- I am not my body.
- I do not need to take care of my body.

Add any other reasons that you can think of to this list, and write them down.

Each time you are about to eat something, ask yourself, "Does my body truly need nourishment from this food right now?"

Your purpose on the Earth is to create authentic power—to align your personality with your soul. It is also to give gifts that your soul desires to contribute to the human experience. As you move in this direction, your life fills with meaning, purpose, clarity, and joy. Love becomes a way of life. As you move away from it, meaning flows out of your life, activities become burdensome chores, and you focus more and more on your own concerns. Your life fills with fear.

The first circumstance is healthy. The second circumstance

is unhealthy. Both circumstances serve the needs of your soul, which are to express harmony, cooperation, sharing, and reverence for Life. The healthy circumstance—authentic power and the contribution of gifts your soul wants to give—allows your soul the full expression it seeks. The unhealthy circumstance brings to your attention inner dynamics that prevent the creation of harmony, cooperation, sharing, and reverence for Life. These dynamics are the release of energy from your energy system in fear and doubt.

FOOD FOR THOUGHT

Say to yourself, "My craving for food will never fill me. I open myself to the possibility that my true nourishment comes from the Universe, and that nourishment is endless."

The difference between the two circumstances is the choices you have made. **When you indulge your anger, jealousy, vengefulness, sorrow, or any other form of fear, you turn your back on the nourishment the Universe provides you.** That nourishment begins with your emotions. Indulging in your emotions—such as shouting in anger, withdrawing in sorrow, striking in rage—is like surrounding yourself with food and not eating. You starve even while food is piled high around you.

Feeling your emotions with the intention to learn from them, and the knowledge that your emotions are gifts from the Universe, is eating at a banquet that never ends. When you indulge painful emotions and do not step back from them enough to see that they serve you, inform you, and

"You starve even while food is piled high around you."

signal you, you are like the ancient mariner, dying of thirst on an ocean of water.

Your emotions tell you how your energy system is functioning at each moment. They show you at which locations energy is leaving your energy system in fear and doubt and where it is leaving in love and trust. Your job is to identify where energy leaves you in fear and doubt, and change what you need to so that it leaves in love and trust.

What you need to change uniquely defines your curriculum in the Earth school. It may be a fear of expressing yourself or a need to control. It may be learning to listen or to speak. It may be caring for others and it may be letting others care for you. It is always a changing combination of challenges that you must confront in order to move in the direction your soul wants to travel. Traveling in the direction your soul wants to go is the creation of authentic power—in other words, spiritual growth, which begins with emotional awareness.

Emotional awareness is the first step in learning how to receive the nourishment the Universe provides for

you. Your energy system always generates emotions. Each is new, even if it is similar to previous emotions. The same fear, or anger, or jealousy does not stay, just as the same water does not stay at one place in a river. No matter how long you watch a river, you never see the same water twice.

The dynamics that produce your fear, anger, jealousy, rage, and despair stay. Changing them changes your emotions. Acting on your emotions by shouting, withdrawing, or striking out indulges your emotions. It prevents you from focusing on your energy system. Water is everywhere, but you do not have a drop to drink.

When you use your emotions to learn how your energy system is processing energy, you ingest the nourishment that the Universe provides. You step back from your emotions. You observe them while you feel them. You experience where you feel sensations in your body, and you notice the thoughts you are thinking.

All this is part of a process that serves your spiritual growth. When you accept this process, embrace it, and use it to learn about what you need to change, you receive nourishment from the Universe. You no longer seek solace in potato chips, fast food, or chocolate. Your diet is complete and you do not need more. The food you eat is no longer a substitute for nourishment from the Universe that your soul longs for. Your longings change from carbohydrates to a fuller, richer life. Nothing can compare to that. Pizza, birthday cake, and chocolate pie all become again what they always were—energy for your body and a treat for your palate.

The size of your body is not the issue. Why you eat is the issue. When you eat to fill a hunger that food cannot satisfy, your body becomes larger than it needs to be. There is no ideal body. There is only your life path through the Earth school unfolding before you from the time of your birth to the moment of your death. There is abundant nutrition along the way—every experience is potential nourishment. Honoring every experience, and every emotion is how you receive that nourishment. When you push your emotions away, you refuse it. **As you learn to receive the nourishment the Universe provides, and you become proficient at receiving it, your body assumes a form that expresses its own balance.**

Eating is sacred. It mirrors the flow of energy that moves through your energy system at each moment. When your energy system functions optimally—when energy is released through each of its centers in love and trust—you move through the Earth school effortlessly and effectively. You naturally create harmony, cooperation, sharing, and reverence for Life. This is the experience of authentic power.

EATING IS SACRED

Every time you eat or drink anything, say to yourself, "Eating is sacred. I eat this food to nourish my body, not to push away the nourishment that only the Universe can provide."

When energy leaves any center in fear and doubt it draws your attention through the creation of painful emotions. You experience painful sensations in the vicinity of the location through which energy is leaving in fear and doubt. You think judgmental thoughts that compare what is with what you think should be. These physical sensations and thoughts, together, form the experience of painful emotions, such as anger, despair, jealousy, or vengefulness. All of these are forms of fear. Each is created by energy leaving your energy system in fear and doubt.

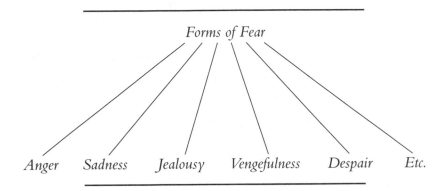

Forms of Fear

Anger   Sadness   Jealousy   Vengefulness   Despair   Etc.

The antidote for painful emotions is love and trust. Changing the way you release energy from your energy system from fear and doubt to love and trust is the healing journey of spiritual transformation. The journey is different for each individual, but the destination for each individual is the same—the conscious and continual release of energy through love and trust rather than through fear and doubt. The release of energy in love and trust produces health, contentment, gratitude, and joy. It brings satisfaction and meaning. It removes the barriers between you and your life. Every experience becomes a friend, even those that are painful. This is the experience of authentic power.

A life on the Earth is an opportunity to create authentic power. It is a dramatic act of spiritual responsibility in which each experience reveals, through the functioning of your energy system, precisely what stands between you and the experience of authentic power. Your painful emotions are your signposts. They bring your attention to what needs to be changed in order for you to create an authentically empowered life—a life in which your personality is aligned with your soul.

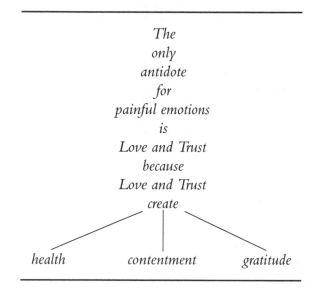

*The
only
antidote
for
painful emotions
is
Love and Trust
because
Love and Trust
create*

health   contentment   gratitude

When you ignore your emotions, you ignore this complex and powerful system, but it never ignores you. **The tension between your efforts to disregard the signals your energy system provides you and the continual flow of these signals to you is the origin of every compulsion, obsession, fixation, and addiction.**

Your attraction to food, and reliance upon it for relief of painful emotions, is an attempt to create the meaningful and satisfying life you were born to create but without doing the necessary work. It is an illusory shortcut that leads to physical dysfunction. It delays the inner work that needs to be done, but does not remove the need to do it.

My emotions are
the best
desserts
for
my
SOUL
and
body.

Until you do this work, you will continue to release energy through your energy system in fear and doubt. Each time you do, a painful emotion brings your attention to what you are doing. Your emotions, including your painful emotions, are friends that come bearing gifts. Each gift is crafted for you by an artisan who knows more about you than you know about yourself. That is what makes every gift precious. Each is a gift of knowledge about yourself.

What is more worthy of your attention—a gift of knowledge about yourself or another cookie?

Sex

YOUR ENERGY SYSTEM PROVIDES you with information continuously about how it is processing energy. That information is your emotions. Obsession with sexual interactions is a way of keeping that information from your awareness.

Every interaction generates emotions. When your focus is on sex, your ability to experience your emotions is reduced or incapacitated. Even the excitement and fear that accompany a potential sexual interaction are hidden behind a screen of fantasy that separates you from the person to whom you feel attracted. This is the experience of an addictive sexual attraction. Locating a potential sexual partner is accompanied by a jolt of excitement and fear that is out of proportion to the occasion. That person may be someone you do not know, or someone whom you have known for a long time. Suddenly, you are excited and frightened by the idea of sex with him or her, and your excitement and fear are surprisingly, sometimes shockingly, intense.

This type of sexual attraction—addictive sexual attraction—is a defense against awareness of the most painful experience in the Earth school—the experience of being powerless. It is the terror of feeling unloved and

*"That is the experience
of being powerless."*

unlovable. It is the fear of being discovered, at your core, to be inadequate and ugly, the fear of being rejected and alone. The stronger these emotions are, when there is no willingness to feel them, the stronger becomes the obsession with sex. An addictive sexual attraction *is* an unwillingness to experience painful emotions.

A sexual addict is an individual in acute pain. She is consumed by feelings of inadequacy. Some sexual addicts are controlled by a need to please others. Some have violent fantasies and explosive anger. Some seek revenge and cannot achieve it. Their lives are empty and lonely. They are resentful and bitter. The pain of each individual is an expression of his or her unique life, and the decisions that he or she has made, but the depth of the pain of anyone in the grip of a sexual addiction is great.

He cannot reach that pain, except when it erupts into his life. She pushes it away, except when despair or resentment floods her awareness. Their lives are series of eruptions and floods, between which they find themselves craving sex, and looking for potential sexual partners. Some individuals act in rage or despair. Others withdraw in rage and despair. Some dive into the drama of their experiences, and others attempt to numb themselves to what they feel.

They cannot rest from thoughts of sex. They move from one encounter to the next. Each sexual experience brings only temporary relief from their craving, and it quickly returns. No amount of sexual activity can satisfy it. That is because their craving is not for sex, but for something deeper, more significant, and more difficult to obtain.

Experiences of addictive sexual attraction can be continual and intense, occupying almost every thought, or they can be in the background of awareness, and only activated by the appearance of a potential sexual partner. A sexual addict sees a potential sexual partner as someone who holds the answer to his most difficult question. She appears to be the substance that he needs to fill his empty life. He appears to have the qualities that she needs to complete her. A sexual addict goes from one person to another on a never-ending search for sexual satisfaction, hoping each time that the next partner will be her or his salvation.

The experience of addictive sexual attraction is a flag that signals a craving for meaning, purpose, and value. This craving lies beneath the sexual craving—it is the controlling impulse. When it is not recognized, it generates irresistible sexual attractions to individuals in the same circumstance. Weakness is drawn to weakness. In fact, each is attracted to the other because of an inner pain that each hopes the other can remove from his or her life. That is why addictive sexual interactions are never satisfying. They are brief moments of relief from sexual craving, but the craving always returns. This is the first clue that there is more involved in addictive sexual attraction than sex.

UNRAVELING A SEXUAL ADDICTION

Stage One—Denial

"I am just a loving person."

"Maybe there is something to look at."

"It's not a problem, but I'll look at it if you're upset about it."

Stage Two—Acceptance

"There is something there."

"This could be a problem."

"All right. Maybe there is a problem."

"Okay. There is a problem."

"This is a big problem."

Stage Three—Opening to Healing

"I am out of control."

An individual who feels powerless—frightened, unwanted, unlovable, and without worth—has an internal radar. This radar scans every room that he enters for a particular target—another individual who feels as powerless as he. When he locates such a person, he feels a sexual attraction. He is not aware of feeling powerless, frightened, unwanted, or unlovable. He feels sexually attracted. He is certain that the person in front of him has activated his attraction. Yet something very different has been ignited within him—the need to use another person to create relief, even if only for a moment, of the pain of feeling frightened, unwanted, without worth, and the other excruciating experiences of powerlessness.

He does not realize that the person to whom he is attracted is his counterpart. He cannot see that she, also, is searching for someone to use in the same way. He cannot see the need to exploit another in himself, so he cannot see that in the other person. He has become her target in the same way she has become his. She is no more interested in him than he is in her.

If he could see clearly, he would be repulsed and so would she. It is one thing to realize that the person you are with means nothing to you, and it is another to realize that you mean nothing to the person with you. His interest in her is limited to the temporary satisfaction of his craving. He cannot see that she has only the same interest in him. He is as replaceable to her as she is to him. They both use one another to feel worthy. This is the dynamic that lies beneath the experience of addictive sexual attraction. It is the central core of human negativity. It is as ugly to see as it is to experience.

An addictive sexual attraction makes pornography magnetically attractive. Images of individuals involved in sexual interactions replace actual sexual interactions when those are not available. The energy of exploitation is the same in both cases. There is no interest in the challenges, fears, vulnerabilities, and joys of another individual. The complexity and difficulties of a human life are ignored. There is no emotional involvement. Attention is focused on satisfying a craving, and on others as potential means of satisfying the craving.

The more intense the pain of fear, unworthiness, and feeling unlovable becomes, the more obsessive becomes the need to have a sexual interaction. When this pain diminishes, the sexual obsession weakens, or temporarily disappears. When an individual becomes stressed again, it returns. This happens to marriage partners as well as to individuals who are not married. When emotional difficulties arise, other people become sexually attractive. The other people are always individuals who are equally powerless. External circumstances do not matter. Intentions matter. When the intention is to exploit another individual, the attraction you feel is an addictive sexual attraction. There is nothing manly, womanly, or healthy about it.

Addictive sexual attraction is a symptom. Painful emotions are the cause of the symptom. A sexual addict is repelled by individuals who are whole and emotionally secure. She cannot find in them what she needs—weaknesses upon which she can prey. Every addictive sexual interaction—including addictive sexual interactions between marriage partners—is motivated by the need to experience, even briefly, power, worthiness, and self-value. The need for self-worth, self-value, and self-appreciation creates the addictive sexual attraction and the fantasies that accompany it.

The sexual attraction is real and powerful, but what lies beneath it is the important issue. Focusing on an addictive sexual attraction, by indulging it or resisting it, avoids the issue. The issue is painful emotions that are calling for attention. Until they are attended, sexual compulsions remain.

An addictive sexual attraction is never to another person. It is an attraction to an image that you hold of another person. You imagine that he or she is attracted to you because of your admirable qualities. You imagine that you are desirable, sexy, and attractive. You imagine that the individual to whom you are attracted puts you on a pedestal, and you feel good on it. None of this is accurate. The person to whom you are attracted holds you in no more esteem than you hold him or her.

If you do not imagine these qualities in yourself, you imagine them in the other person. You imagine that he is desirable, sexy, and attractive. You put him or her on a pedestal, and you feel secure doing that. This is not accurate, either. The person to whom you are attracted does not hold himself or herself in esteem any more than you honor yourself.

That is why addictive sexual interactions are barriers to intimacy, even though they appear to be intimate. How is intimacy possible when individuals involved are exploiting one another? How can any of them be vulnerable, share what is important, explore their feelings, and appreciate the other?

They cannot because addictive sexual interactions are encounters in which the participants do not care about each other. Addictive sexual interaction is an arena devoid of empathy and tenderness. Each participant sees his or her partner as interchangeable with other sexual partners. Each is a fix to each other, just as alcohol is a fix to an alcoholic, and heroin to a heroin addict. Each sexual addict is both predator and prey, seducer and seduced. Each feeds on the other.

A sexual addiction is difficult to see in yourself. The more painful the emotions underlying the addiction, the more difficult the addiction is to discover. Sexual addiction is the most pervasive addiction in the human experience. Every impulse to satisfy a craving through the exploitation of another person is generated by a deeper and more potent craving—the craving to live a fulfilling life of meaning and purpose. The frustration of this craving is the origin of every painful emotion.

EMOTIONS AND SEXUAL ADDICTION

If you feel you are sexually addicted and you want to find the origin of this addiction, it is important to be gentle with yourself.

Remember the last time you were sexually attracted to someone. Remember how you felt—excitement at the thought of having sex with him or her. Were you also aware of your fear?

Stay with that time. Do a scan of your energy system. What are you feeling? Where are you feeling it? What thoughts are accompanying your physical sensations?

The next time you meet someone you are attracted to sexually, go deeper than the excitement and fear you feel about a sexual interaction with this person. Scan your energy system. Allow yourself to feel your attraction. Allow yourself also to feel what is beneath it instead of acting on it.

An individual who lives a fulfilling and meaningful life is not tormented by fears and vulnerabilities. She has no need to defend herself or criticize another. He does not require the admiration of others, or feel the need to admire others. His creativity is in the present moment. He is excited by his life, not frightened of it. All that he says and does is appropriate. His days are filled with joy, even when difficult experiences occur. His nights are restful and refreshing. This is the experience of authentic power.

Painful emotions have causes. These causes are internal, not external. Avoiding painful emotions prevents the exploration of their causes. Without awareness of their causes, their causes cannot be changed, and painful emotions remain. **Connecting the experience of addictive sexual attraction with the avoidance of painful emotions is a significant step in healing an addiction to sex.** It is a connection that needs to be examined at depth in order for the emotional pain that lies beneath every addictive sexual attraction to be healed. The only alternative to making this connection, and exploring it, is to continue the pursuit of addictive sexual interactions, leaving the emotions beneath the addiction buried.

Burying painful emotions is like burying dynamite. They will explode. The emotions that lie beneath addictive sexual attractions are painful. They are anger, rage, frustration, jealousy, despair, vengefulness, and every other form of fear. Each is a different flower on the same plant. The root of the plant is fear— the experience of powerlessness.

Loving sexual intimacy is a different dynamic. It expresses care and appreciation. It is mutual giving, not mutual taking. It is an arena in which individuals nurture each other rather than exploit each other. **In loving sexual intimacy, sexual partners are not interchangeable.** They are unique in their histories, aptitudes, struggles, and joys. They know each other and care for each other. They empathize. They are interested in each other. They use physical intimacy to deepen their emotional intimacy. They laugh with each other. They pay attention to what they feel. They are committed to growing together. Their sexual interactions are sacred to them, and they are sacred to each other.

It is impossible to have a sexual interaction without deepening the emotional connection between the partners. This emotional deepening has no channel for expression in addictive sexual interactions. When it is not expressed, it eventually creates psychological and physical dysfunctions which, in turn, contribute to the reservoir of painful emotions that generate addictive sexual attraction.

Every addictive sexual attraction—every powerful jolt of excitement and fear—to a person whom you do not know, or with whom you do not desire to deepen your emotional connection, or whose history, fears, aspirations, joys, and struggles do not interest you, or about whom you do not care deeply, is a flight from the experience of painful emotions. Even marriage partners, when they engage one another in addictive sexual interactions, are fleeing from the experience of painful emotions.

Every addictive sexual attraction is resistance to emotional awareness.

PART III

Common Themes

Power Struggles

OWER STRUGGLES ARE ANTIQUES IN THE MAKING.
They are becoming dated, and eventually they will become obsolete. The difference between power struggles
and antiques is that antiques acquire nostalgic value, but power
struggles will not. They will be seen clearly for what they are—
artifacts of an earlier form of human evolution that is no longer
constructive.

When a new structure is built, excavation of the building
site unearths rusted pipe, bent nails, broken glass, and founda-
tions of buildings built long ago. Ground is now being broken
for a new human awareness. When this structure is complete, it
will replace all that stood in the same place. A new humankind
is being born, and with it a new consciousness that is changing
every aspect of the human experience.

Power struggles are the most prominent characteristic of
the human experience, the dominant elements in the landscape. Human history is the chronicle of power struggles
between individuals, tribes, races, religions, the sexes, and nations. Every country and culture has its stories of struggles with
other countries and cultures. Every neighbor has similar stories.
Every power struggle is an expression of an understanding
upon which human experience has been built until now—

the understanding of power as the ability to manipulate and control.

Nations fight with each other for the same reason that children fight with each other. They want control. Cain killed Abel for the same reason that every homicide occurs—the need to control. Taking life is the most extreme expression of the dynamic that underlies every argument and conflict, whether it is between parents, children, classmates, or colleagues. It is the attempt to manipulate or control.

Striving to manipulate and control what appears to be external, including other people, is the pursuit of external power. Creating external power has kept the human species alive, and allowed it to prosper. It has produced shelter, agriculture, science, and spacecraft. Everything that does not occur naturally is a product of external power, such as this book, the chair that you are sitting in, the car that transports you, the phone that connects you, and the clothes that you wear.

The story of human evolution until now and the pursuit of external power are the same story. It has been a glorious story, except when we pursued external power without reverence. That is the origin of every violence in the human experience. The pursuit of external power without reverence is the cause of every conflict, cruelty, and painful emotion.

Reverence is appreciation of the sacred. It is a holy perception. It is seeing beyond the shell of form and into essence. It is valuing everything because it is. Reverence is an appreciation of Life in all of its forms, the realization that there is nothing but Life.

The pursuit of external power without reverence has devastated the Earth, destroyed cultures, starved children, and surrounded us with brutality. **The pursuit of external power without reverence produces one thing—power struggles.**

*"The pursuit of external power
without reverence produces
one thing—power struggles."*

With or without reverence, the pursuit of external power now leads only to violence and destruction. It is an evolutionary modality that no longer works. It is the wrong medicine, and nothing can make it the right medicine again. The understanding of power as the ability to manipulate and control is not negative, just as the development of electricity did not make candles negative. It is obsolete. This obsolete perception is now counterproductive in every way.

Using candles instead of lights is inefficient. Candlepower is incapable of supporting technologically advanced societies. Pursuing external power is more than inefficient. It is dangerous. The pursuit of external power is no longer an option that is compatible with the survival of humanity. Even the pursuit of external power with reverence is no longer an option. The pursuit of external power has no future, and neither does any relationship or social structure built upon it.

There are no constructive consequences that can come from a power struggle, because the perception of power as the ability to manipulate and control no longer serves human evolution. That perception underlies every power struggle.

Hoarding, competition, discord, and exploitation are consequences of pursuing external power without reverence. **In a power struggle, your desire to manipulate and control others conflicts with their desire to manipulate and control you.** The issue may appear to be who is right and who is wrong or which thought is true and which is false. It never is. The issue is always external power. External power can be gained and lost, just as elections are won and lost, and market share increases and decreases. Every election is a power struggle. The winner acquires external power—the ability to manipulate and control. Every competition is a power struggle. The business that captures more market acquires more external power—the ability to manipulate and control.

Each tennis, golf, and bowling match is a power struggle when winning is the objective. Every football, baseball, and basketball game is a power struggle when only victory can give value to the victor, and every defeat brings pain. Striving to manipulate and control in order to make yourself feel more valuable, worthy, admirable, and lovable is the pursuit of external power. Striving to do your best for the joy of expressing all that you have to contribute is a satisfying experience that does not depend upon the outcome. **When the outcome is more important to you than the activity, you are in a power struggle.**

Authentically empowered people live in homes, eat, and wear clothes, too, but they do not use their homes, clothes, or technology to make themselves feel safer or more valuable than other people or other forms of Life. They use everything to create harmony, cooperation, sharing, and reverence for Life. These are the intentions of the soul.

Reading books and using computers in order to contribute to Life, not exploit Life, is the pursuit of authentic power. Cooperating to create harmony, not conflict, is the pursuit of authentic power. Growing food to share, not to survive, is the pursuit of authentic power.

ARE YOU IN A POWER STRUGGLE?

How do you know you are in a power struggle?
   Ask yourself these questions:

   Am I feeling right?

   Am I certain the other person is wrong?

   Am I feeling hurt?

   Am I feeling angry?

   Am I impatient?

   Am I blaming others?

   Am I feeling distance from another person?

   Am I attached to an outcome?

   Do I want to win?

   If your answer to any of these questions is yes, you are in a power struggle.

Power struggles occur because the participants feel powerless and they choose to pursue external power. Power struggles can only occur between individuals who are pursuing external power. They seek to control each other. They are in pain. That pain is the pain of powerlessness. Instead of experiencing that pain, they reach outward in an attempt to rearrange the world. They become thinner, richer, more educated or skilled. They get married or divorced. They cut their hair long or short, or braid it or straighten it. They smile, cry, withdraw, or rage according to how they have learned to create external power.

The pain of powerlessness results from energy leaving your energy system in fear and doubt. You can identify your fears and doubts by the physical pain that occurs in the vicinity of particular centers in your energy system. Physical pain in the vicinity of your solar plexus (third center) is produced by fears that you cannot provide for yourself, defend yourself, or do what you need to do. Painful sensations in your chest (fourth center) are produced when you fear that you cannot love or be loved. You obstruct the flow of love to and from you. Tightness in your throat, or dysfunction there, tells you that you fear to express yourself, and so on. Every center produces particular sensations when energy leaves it in fear and doubt. All of them are painful.

STOPPING THE STRUGGLE

Think of the last time you were in a power struggle—with your mate, co-worker, member of your family, or a stranger. Get it clearly in your mind. Think about it until you begin to feel the way you did then. Let yourself feel your physical sensations and where they are. What thoughts are you thinking as you feel these sensations?

The next time you find yourself in a power struggle, do the same thing. Take a time-out so you can feel what you are feeling in your body and where. Notice the thoughts you are thinking. Allow yourself to be more interested in the physical sensations you are feeling in your body, and where you are feeling them, than you are in the struggle.

Each student in the Earth school walks a unique path. All have fears to confront and doubts to challenge. Power struggles are ways of avoiding fears and challenges. They obstruct emotional awareness. An individual in pain becomes angry instead of experiencing painful sensations in his body. She feels slighted. He becomes righteous. Whatever the reaction, it is an attempt to manipulate and control. Rather than experience a painful emotion, an argument begins, or a pushing match, or a war. The dynamic is the same for individuals and for collectives. **The pursuit of external power is always an attempt to avoid pain.**

Looking inward rather than outward, finding the source of pain and changing it into a source of gratitude is the pursuit of authentic power. Authentic power is the alignment of the personality with the soul. **Creating authentic power is using your will to change your life, not the lives of others.** It is recognizing that you have a purpose on the Earth, finding it, and living it.

Power struggles take each participant away from awareness

"Each student in the Earth school walks a unique path."

of what is necessary to heal the pain of powerlessness. They are attempts to feel powerful, even for a moment, by dominating another person.

When you hold the intention to create harmony instead of discord, sharing instead of hoarding, cooperation instead of competition, and reverence for Life instead of exploitation of Life—the intentions of your soul—power struggles are impossible. Creating these goals begins with experiencing the painful emotions that produce power struggles.

That is emotional awareness. Every power struggle is a flight from emotional awareness. Anger, rage, jealousy, vengefulness, and fear are so painful that, instead of experiencing them, you shout, accuse, blame, or withdraw in order to manipulate and control another person. Every participant in a power struggle is frightened and hurting. Refusing to experience that fear and pain perpetuates the struggle. A power struggle is the process of ignoring painful emotions.

There are as many ways to struggle for external power as there are individuals who struggle. Some shout or scream, and some brood. Some hold grudges, and some gossip. Some withdraw emotionally, while some withhold affection. Some smile and others cry.

All create distance. A power struggle does not depend on behavior. It depends upon intention. The intention to manipulate and control creates a power struggle when it meets the same intention. **A power struggle collapses when you withdraw your energy from it.** It cannot continue without your intention to manipulate and control. When your intention is to observe your inner processes, everything changes. You withdraw energy from the struggle. Your attention is on your emotions.

When your goal is to heal the pain within you that creates

your need to control and manipulate, you are no longer interested in manipulating and controlling. This is the way to challenge an impulse to be righteous, right, stronger, smarter, or louder. **Power struggles become uninteresting to you when you change your intention from winning to learning about yourself.** Self-awareness becomes important. Intimacy is the goal.

POWER STRUGGLE VERSUS INTIMACY

Power Struggle	Intimacy
Emotionally closed.	Vulnerable
Right, righteous	Compassionate
Walled off	Open heart
Controlling	Cooperative
Win at all costs	Win-win
Territorial	Shares
Blames others	Self-responsible
Discord	Harmony
Avoids pain	Wants to heal
Resists fear	Faces fear
Self-concerned	Self-aware
Seeks external power	Seeks authentic power
Spiritually stagnant	Spiritually growing
Attached to outcome	Detached from outcome
Rearranging outer world.	Changing inner world

Power struggles prevent intimacy. You doubt that you can control and manipulate another individual. You fear that she will not think, speak, or act as you desire. This fear is the root of the power struggle. The creation of authentic power requires the intention to cooperate with everyone, not only those who share your goals. It requires the intention to create harmony with everyone, not only those who admire you. It requires the intention to share with everyone, not only those who share with you. It requires the intention to revere Life in all of its forms, not only those that do not threaten you.

Power struggles illuminate dynamics within you that you must change in order to create authentic power. They show you the work that you need to do. They are guideposts on your journey. Each points to a place that you need to locate and change. When you do, guideposts no longer point to that place.

Eventually, guideposts will be unnecessary.

Savior Searching

THE SEARCH FOR SALVATION takes place outside of your interior experience. **Savior searching is the effort to locate an individual or circumstance that can deliver you from your discomfort.** The search may be for a perfect mate, home, job, or automobile. It may be for money, fame, education, a slim or muscular body. The salvation appears to come from different sources for different people. In no case does the salvation come from within.

Romantic attraction is the experience of locating a savior. She has everything that you need to complete your life. He is charming, strong, handsome, and capable. She is warm, caring, gracious, and lovely. The attraction is to the capability that the individual has to solve your problems, eliminate your inner struggles, and bring your experience to a new level of comfort.

"She has everything that you need to complete your life."

The breakdown of romantic attraction—the end of the honeymoon—begins when the savior cannot deliver. Since both individuals in a romantic attraction view the other as a savior, this disillusionment is shared. Each sees in the other characteristics that were not visible previously, such as a quick temper, melancholy inclination, fear of expression, insensitivities, and vulnerabilities. These characteristics were present throughout the romantic attraction. As they become visible, the illusion of salvation in the form of another individual begins to unravel.

The more it unravels, the more the discomforts that occupied your attention before the romantic attraction reappear. Your life continues, but with the addition of a companion. Your jealousy, fear of people, anger, and self-doubt return. They disappeared during the romantic attraction. The promise of salvation—like a morning fog—obscured them, but did not remove them. When the fog evaporated, they were still there. They will continue to be there until you address them.

The search for salvation takes your attention away from what you feel and places it on external circumstances. Emotional awareness is put aside. Your anticipation of a life without pain temporarily replaces the pain that you feel. That is the power of a romantic attraction—the promise of permanent release from pain.

It is also the power of a job that you have yet to obtain, house that you have yet to own, or dress that you have yet to buy. You focus on creating the career, owning the house, or buying the dress. You run from your emotions. The harder you run, the more promising the career becomes. The more the house appears to be the answer to your difficulties, the more attractive the dress becomes. When you have the career, the house, or the dress, the honeymoon ends. Your anxieties, fears, resentment and self-doubt return, and you begin the search for salvation again.

Another job or house calls to you. You buy another dress. You find another romantic attraction. Each time, you divert your attention from your emotions. You place it on objects, including other people. You seek your salvation in them. **You place upon your saviors the responsibility for doing the work that only you can do.** Your work remains undone.

THE SAVIOR SEARCH

When you feel you may be looking for a savior again, stop and feel what you are feeling. Then ask yourself this question, "Do I feel this person, situation, or thing is the answer to my well-being?"

This is the pursuit of external power. You achieve, dress, and speak to influence others. You strive to manipulate and control them through your appearance, the things that you own, your skills, aptitudes, and accomplishments. You value yourself only as much as they value you. When others do not approve of you, your sense of well-being diminishes or disappears. When they appreciate you, you feel grand. Romantic attraction mutually fulfills the need of both participants to be appreciated. It allows them to feel buoyant. They appear to themselves as attractive. They feel sexual. Their walk is lighter, they laugh more easily, and they enjoy their lives.

When the romance ends, they plummet into despair and self-doubt. They rage or withdraw. These, also, are attempts to manipulate and control. They hope to regain the affection that they have lost, and the self-image that accompanied it. External power can be lost, gained, inherited, earned, and won. It comes and goes. She loves me; she loves me not. The difference is joy and exuberance on the one hand and pain on the other.

Every attempt to place your salvation in the hands of another individual is an attempt to escape from painful emotions. You relinquish responsibility for your emotions and their creation. You look upon yourself as a victim and depend upon someone or something to save you. You see your painful emotions as punishment, unjust or random. You attempt to separate your intentions, thoughts, words, and actions from your emotional experiences.

Your emotions are designed to bring your attention to internal dynamics that need to be changed. These are the dynamics that produce your fear, anger, vengefulness, jealousy, and sorrow. These emotions are products of your energy system that show you how energy is processed in that system, and where. When you distract yourself with the pursuit of a savior, this information continues to be produced, energy continues to be processed, and emotions continue to be painful.

The search for a savior provides a brief respite from your experience of these painful dynamics, but it does not change them. Only changing the way that energy is processed in your energy system from fear and doubt to love and trust can change the emotions that you experience. When you ignore your emotions, you ignore the information that you need to change them. **When you place as much attention on what you are feeling in your body as you put on the search for a savior, you become your own salvation.** You look inward instead of outward. What you find is the pain that drove you to seek salvation in an individual or a circumstance.

EXPLORING YOUR SAVIORS

Make a list of your saviors. For example:

A new partner

A new job

A new car

A new dress

Money

Education

Fame

Explore each savior on your list, one by one. Remember how you felt when you wanted it. Were you excited? Were you scared? Go deeper and scan your energy system. Where do you feel physical sensations in your body, and what do you feel?

Remember when you got your savior. Were you excited? Did you feel "on top of the world"? How long did it last? Now go deeper into your feelings. Notice what physical sensations you feel in your body, and where you feel them.

Now remember when the honeymoon ended—the dress, the house, the partner, the car looked ordinary again. How long did the honeymoon last? How did you feel when it was over? Notice what physical sensations you feel in your body, and where you feel them.

Pain in your chest tells you that energy is leaving that center (fourth) in fear and doubt. Your heart is closed. You judge and compare individuals. You are more interested in accomplishments and possessions than you are in people. Healing the pain in your chest requires forgiving. Anger feeds the pain, while appreciation soothes it. Judging others tightens your chest, while blessing them loosens it. No savior can forgive for you. Only you can give your blessings, and only your blessings can ease the pain in your heart.

Pain near your solar plexus tells you that energy is leaving that center (third) in fear and doubt. You fear that you cannot support yourself. You need the approval of others. You are frightened of rejection. Your self-worth depends upon the evaluation of others, and you doubt your ability. Healing this pain requires changing those perceptions. It requires examining your assumptions. More than ulcers, indigestion, and back spasms are at issue. It is your unexamined assumptions about yourself and your fear that you are incapable of meeting the challenges of your life.

Instead of experiencing the painful emotions that fear and doubt create, you search for an individual or circumstance that you feel is the answer to your questions, the solution to your problems, and the source of your happiness. You are the source of your happiness. It is not a gift that is bestowed upon you, or a treasure that you find. It is a creation and you are the only one who can create it.

MY HAPPINESS

Say to yourself, "I am the only one who can create happiness in my life. The source of my happiness is within me."

"You are the source of your happiness."

Your painful emotions tell you what needs to be changed in you, not in other people. They call your attention to your energy system. Your energy system produces physical sensations. The type of sensation, painful or pleasing, depends upon the way energy is processed at each location in your energy system—through fear and doubt or through love and trust.

Your emotions are dependable and accurate information that keeps you current on the functioning of your energy system. To change your emotions, you must change the way energy is processed. The shift from fear and doubt to love and trust is the shift that each moment in the Earth school supports. Painful emotions are part of that support.

You do not need to be saved from your painful emotions any more than you need to be saved from a messenger who brings you news that can create your health. While you search for a savior, you run from the messenger, and your news goes undelivered.

Judging

WHEN YOU JUDGE, you shift attention away from yourself and onto others. By focusing on what is external you keep your attention away from what is occurring inside of you.

Judging others is a way of attempting to change the world, or reorder it to your approval. It is a hemorrhage of energy—in other words, a loss of power. You lose power to the people and circumstances that you judge. They occupy your thoughts and your attention. You are mesmerized by them, much as you are by a movie that captivates your attention.

When you judge others, you forget who you are, what your goals and desires are, and, most important, what you are feeling. The impulse to judge others is a ticket to a movie that you have seen before and that still attracts you. When you act on the impulse, you enter the theater. In the movie that is playing, you are superior to others and you have the right to impose your will upon them. Actually, your attention is not on others because you do not care about what they are thinking or feeling. You are not interested in their struggles or accomplishments. Their histories are of no importance to you, and you do not see them as companions, colleagues in the Earth school, or even as individuals. You see only what is objectionable to you—what makes you feel uncomfortable.

The impulse to judge is generated by internal pain. It is more than a psychological impulse. Behind the impulse to judge is a physical pain that would be extremely uncomfortable to experience. Rather than experience it, you act on the impulse and judge. Your attention goes to a behavior that you do not like, clothes that do not please you, or a voice that is too loud or too soft. You label others.

Most people do not realize that behind the impulse to judge circumstances and people is a physical pain. As they hold others in contempt, or rage at them, they hide their own discomfort from themselves. Until they are able to feel that discomfort, become familiar with it, and challenge it, they will compulsively find fault with circumstances and with others.

THINK OF A TIME

Think of a time when you judged someone, and you are still holding onto that judgment. What were you saying about him or her then, and what do you say about him or her now?

Scan your energy system. What physical sensations are you feeling, and where in your body are you feeling them? Allow yourself to feel the pain you were trying to cover up by judging someone else. Be gentle with yourself.

When an individual agrees to change in order to satisfy your criteria, your relief is temporary. The need to change the world and others—to judge—does not originate in the external world. It is a product of an inner imbalance. That need remains until the imbalance is corrected.

Indulging in a compulsion, including the compulsion to judge, is like taking a pill to dull a pain. How many pills have you taken today? How many did you take yesterday? How many did you take last month? How many have you taken over the last year? If each time you judged someone actually were a pill, how many bottles of them have you consumed? If you are taking that much pain suppressant, how much pain must you be feeling?

The issue is not the pain but what is causing it. Until the cause is discovered, permanent relief is not possible, and the compulsion continues. Treating the symptom will not heal what produces it. The first step in freeing yourself from this destructive dependency is to become aware of your pain and where it occurs—how energy in your energy system is being processed and where.

It is easy to become aware of pain in your body when you are taking pain suppressants. Stop taking them. In the case of your impulse to judge, the result will be immediate. You do not have to wait for the effects of the last pill to wear off. When you frustrate the compulsion to judge, you instantly feel the underlying pain that generates the compulsion. **Frustrating the impulse means stopping what you are doing, including judging, and feel what you feel.** If you do not feel anything, be patient. The pain is there. You will know that it is there if you feel the urge to judge continue—if you continue to see objectionable things about your circumstances or others.

If you feel discomfort and then begin to judge again, be patient with yourself. Take one step at a time. Ease into the awareness of what you experience in your body. This landscape may be new to your awareness, but it has existed since you were born. Your compulsion to judge is a plant that has been growing. Challenging the impulse to judge is like weeding the landscape. Becoming aware of interior experiences—including the pain in your body—is the first step in pulling the plant by the roots.

When you judge others you judge yourself. You attempt to avoid the pain of that judgment by thinking you are judging others. This complex method of avoiding what you feel is a refusal to look at characteristics of yourself that you do not approve. The idea that these characteristics exist in you is painful or shameful. You cannot even imagine that. Your contempt for those characteristics finds expression when you recognize them in someone else. You become angry, frightened, frustrated, or disappointed in another rather than with yourself. This is the origin of judgment.

If you did not possess the characteristics you disdain so, you would have no emotional reaction to them. You would recognize deceit, greed, lust, insensitivity, and every other inadequacy for what it is, and act accordingly. You would not trust an untrustworthy individual, and you would not expect sensitivity where none exists. You would do these things effortlessly. Your emotional reaction to certain characteristics and not others is your signal. When you receive the signal—when you judge another individual—it is because you have recognized in someone else a characteristic that you have not yet identified in yourself.

Until you can acknowledge that you possess the same characteristics you judge harshly in others, you will become enraged, disappointed, angry, and contemptuous

when you see them in others. The longer you deny them, the more prominent they become. At the same time, the more judgmental you become of them in others. Individuals will appear in your life, or reappear, who upset you. You will judge them until you finally realize that your discontent—judgment— for so many of your fellow students in the Earth school is discontent with and harsh judgment of yourself. Then you will be able to change those characteristics in yourself.

The clergyman who battled prostitution and got photographed with a prostitute is an example. His contempt of sexual exploitation was sincere. His battle against it was vigorous, but he fought it on the wrong battlefield. The impulse to exploit others sexually was in him. The more he ignored it, the stronger it became and the more determined became his battle against it in others.

Eventually a compulsion to have sex with a prostitute overwhelmed him—the very thing that he most condemned. When he was discovered, he appeared to be a hypocrite. He was not. He did not recognize the origin of the impulse that he so detested. It originated in himself, and he detested himself. If he did not, he would not detest others with the same impulse. He would see sexual exploitation for what it is—a painful experience of powerlessness—and act accordingly.

Can you consider the possibility that what you judge harshly in others you do yourself, or would like to do? If you can, you are in for a surprise. You will begin to sympathize with others rather than condemn them. You will join humanity as a sensitive and concerned member rather than a critical one. You cannot understand the pain of others until you have felt your own. When you can appreciate your own, you can appreciate the pain of others.

CATCH YOURSELF

When you find yourself judging, stop. Scan your energy system. Notice in your body where you are feeling physical sensations and what sensations you are feeling. Also notice the thoughts you are thinking. Then ask yourself, "What am I not allowing myself to see about myself?"

The pain that produces judgment is a physical experience. **Judgment shifts awareness from the experiences of your body onto the activities of your mind.** When you judge another person, your attention focuses on thoughts about others, but your pain remains—the pain that it is created by energy leaving your energy system in fear and doubt.

The impulse to judge others is your signal that attention needs to be directed inward. It informs you of issues with yourself that are unresolved. Resolving them is your business—not resolving the issues of other people. When you judge others you run from the self-exploration that you are given.

A judge assesses circumstances. Her assessment is limited by preestablished rules—the law. Your judgments of other people are assessments that you make in accordance with your preestablished rules—the laws that you obey. Judging is an attempt to make others obey your laws, too.

Your laws are your beliefs about how you and others should think, appear, speak, and act. They are also your beliefs about the Universe, how it should be, and what your relationship with it should be. When your laws are broken, you condemn others, yourself, and the Universe.

It is painful to see your laws disobeyed. Judging those who disobey them is a way of not feeling that pain. It does not remove the pain, and it also does not remove the cause of the pain. You enter a mental domain where awareness of your painful sensations cannot follow. The more pain you feel, the stronger becomes your need to judge—to avoid the pain you are feeling.

Your energy system functions whether you pay attention to it or not. To stop the pain that creates the compulsion to judge—or drink alcohol, overwork, buy, have sex, eat, or exercise—requires changing the way energy is processed as it moves through your energy system. To do that, you must become aware of how and where that happens. This is exactly what judging others or circumstances prevents you from doing.

Judging others is like focusing your attention into a narrow beam, and directing it away from what you need to see because you do not want to see it. You would rather illuminate less painful images—your perceptions of the inadequacies of others or the unfairness of the Universe. All else remains in darkness, including the painful origins of your perceptions.

Judging prevents you from revealing yourself to yourself and others. It is a barrier against vulnerability. Judging is a continual offensive in a war against your painful experiences of others or the Universe.

Judging prevents intimacy and the emotions that intimate relationships activate. It is a defense against fear, feeling inadequate, and longing for meaning and companionship. **Judging is a preemptive attack against what you most want—intimacy and acceptance—that you launch before you can be rejected or refused intimacy.**

Every judgment is an outpouring of fear and the pain of experiencing it. When you judge continually, that outpouring becomes a river of energy that you could have used to shape your life in meaningful and fulfilling ways. Your judgments of others, yourself, and the Universe will not stop until the pain that creates them is healed, and that requires becoming aware of it.

The pain you are avoiding is the key you are searching for. It is your connection to the immense suffering of humanity and the Earth, and the doorway to your compassion.

Beyond Stress

STRESS IS THE CONSEQUENCE OF RESISTANCE. It is not caused by circumstances in your life. It is not caused by the painful emotions you experience, either. It is caused by your resistance to your life. It is possible for you to encounter a wide variety of circumstances, but it is your resistance to those circumstances that causes stress.

When you resist a circumstance in your life, it takes energy and that produces stress. It is one thing to observe a circumstance and it is another thing to resist it. Challenging and changing a circumstance and resisting it are different. Challenging a situation is using your will to change what you are experiencing—to change the dynamic within yourself that is producing the situation. Resisting is wishing in that moment that you were not experiencing it. It is attempting to stop the experience.

This is important to understand because you will not be able to effectively change a circumstance in your life while you are resisting it. Resisting anything requires energy, and that loss of energy is stress. **The amount of stress in your life is determined by how much energy you expend resisting your life.**

The more you resist your circumstances, the more stress you bring into your life. If you resist everything, your life fills with

274

stress. It becomes a study in stress because it becomes an exercise in resistance. You do not like your job. You do not like your family. You do not like your classmates. You do not like yourself. Nothing that you see or encounter meets your approval. This is a recipe for illness. It is guaranteed to produce painful emotional and physical dysfunctions. If you resist these experiences, you add yet more stress to your life, and your emotional and physical dysfunctions become more intense.

STRESSED OUT?

Write down everything you can think of that you feel stressed about, for example:

- **My mate's habits**
- **Lack of time**
- **Color of my car**
- **My child's behavior**
- **My parents**
- **My boss**
- **My busy schedule**

Save this list.

When you accept the circumstances in your life, you do not squander your energy resisting them. **Resistance is the loss of energy that results when you attempt, with your thoughts and your feelings, to change a person, event, or circumstance.** You reach out with your energy to make that person, or experience, different than it is.

STRESSED OUT

Go back to your list of circumstances, things, and people that you feel stressed about. Consider each of the items on it, one at a time. For each item, scan your energy system. What physical sensations are you feeling and where are they located? Write down what you discover. (Is energy leaving your energy system in love and trust or in fear and doubt?)

Then say to yourself, "These are the circumstances, things, and people that I resist in my life, and my resistance to them is what causes my stress."

No amount of energy can change the circumstances in your life in the moment that you experience them, or the people with whom you interact. There is no if or but to that. When a circumstance in your life does not meet your approval, it is nonetheless what it is. You lose energy by resisting it, and the consequence is the experience of stress.

You may be able to influence future events, or the way individuals interact with you in the future, but that is another story—the story of the pursuit of external power: the ability to manipulate and control. That, also, is an expenditure of energy that cannot produce a constructive consequence.

Attempting to change circumstances or behavior through manipulation and control always produces results that are violent and destructive—that are painful. Stress is your indication that you are resisting your experience in the present moment. Your resistance to your experience is futile and costly. It costs you your health and your ability to create constructively. It keeps you confined to a smaller, more constricted, less satisfying, and less productive life. It prevents you from expanding into the fuller potential that is your joy and your fulfillment.

Resisting the circumstances of your life is the same as saying to a river, "You should not be flowing here. You should be flowing over there." The more you distress yourself over the course of the river, the more energy you lose. You see the river and where it is flowing. You do not like what you see.

Resistance is the second part of this equation: You do not like what you see. Seeing the river and where it flows does not produce stress. Not liking what you see does. Not liking what you see is a loss of energy, not the sight of the river. The flowing river is what you see. The rest is what you add to what you see. When you add dislike, distrust, fear, disdain, disapproval, or any other judgment, you lose energy. That loss of energy is the experience of stress.

Accepting the river as it flows is relief from stress. Relief from stress is freedom. It is the ability to breathe deeply and enjoy the river. It is relaxing into the present moment. The pres-

"...breathe deeply and enjoy the river."

ent moment cannot be divided into parts. When you resist any-thing, you resist the present moment. The present moment is the entirety of your experience. No experience exists outside of the present moment. Memories, regrets, fantasies, and content-ment all exist in the present moment. Anger, judgment, disdain, fear, joy, appreciation, and love also exist in the present moment. Every experience that you have, no matter what it is, exists in the present moment.

When you resist anything that you experience, you resist the present moment. When you resist the present moment, you re-sist your life. When you resist your life, you create stress.

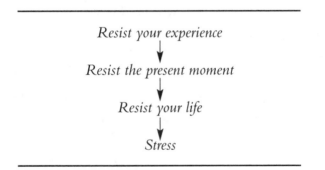

Resist your experience

Resist the present moment

Resist your life

Stress

Accepting the present moment does not mean that you can-not change your life. On the contrary, it allows you to see clearly what needs to be changed. Changing your life is a journey. To make that journey you must travel from where you are to where you want to go. You cannot get to where you want to go unless you know where you are.

Not accepting your life and wanting to change it is like wanting to travel to Chicago but not knowing if you are in Los Angeles or Amsterdam. You cannot get there because you do not know which way to go. Accepting your life allows you to know where you are. When you know where you are, you know which direction you need to travel in order to get where you want to go.

To change your life you must accept your life. This appears to be a paradox but it is not. **Once you accept your life— greet it without resistance—you can determine what you need to change in order to create the circumstances and experiences that you desire.** While you resist your circumstances and experiences, they repulse you, disturb you, and agitate you. You want to change them, but you cannot know how to do that. Your situation is the same as wanting to travel to Chicago but not knowing where you are. You know only that wherever you are, you do not like it.

Accepting your life means being present in it, moment by moment. Changing your life begins with accepting your life as it is. When you do that, you are in a position to change. You know where you are, in addition to where you want to go.

Imagine that you are with a person who is dishonest. It is one thing to see that this person is dishonest. That allows you to

"To change your life you must accept your life."

take appropriate measures. It is another thing to resist his dishonesty. That is where the stress comes in. If you resist his dishonesty, you want to change him. You judge him, evaluate him, and compare him with others. All of these activities are stressful.

When you resist your emotions you create stress. You cannot change your emotions as they move through you. They have their own dynamics. When an emotion appears, it appears for a reason. It will not go away because you do not like it. Your resistance to it causes stress.

MOVING BEYOND

Return again to your list of circumstances, things, and people that you feel stressed about. Consider each of the items on it, one at a time, and as you do, say to yourself, "I open to the possibility that I can accept this circumstance, thing, or person the way it or he or she is." Spend some time really opening to this possibility.

Does this change the physical sensations in your body, and where you are feeling them?

The first step in changing the dynamic that creates an emotion is to experience the emotion. Resisting an emotion prevents you from exploring it. When you accept your emotions, they flow through you like air through a flute. You feel them, which allows you to learn from them. They show you where energy leaves your energy system and how. Your emotions are friends who bring news that you need to know. Resisting them closes the door to that news. It also produces stress.

Accepting your emotions and learning about your energy

system are the same thing. Your emotions inform you about your energy system, and your energy system produces your emotions. Once you understand your energy system and your emotions, you can change how your energy system functions. That is the change from learning through fear and doubt to learning through love and trust.

This change requires paying attention to the sensations in your body. It requires becoming aware of what you feel at each center in your energy system. That is emotional awareness.

Resistance to your life is lack of trust in the Universe. You approve of some of your experiences, but not all of them. When you do not approve, energy leaves you in fear and doubt. You insist on the perceptions, values, and goals of your personality. You ignore the perceptions, values, and goals of your soul. This is painful. Your journey through the Earth school provides you with opportunities to align your personality with your soul. These opportunities continue from the time you are born until the time you die. When you use them to align your personality with your soul, you create authentic power.

Authentic power is freedom from fear and awareness of your creative power as a soul. It is appreciation of the wisdom and compassion of the Universe. That is a life without stress. You value your experiences, use them to guide you in the creation of authentic power, and all the while you do not resist the process.

The process includes resistance. When you accept your life, you accept all that you experience. You accept your resistance, also. You become, at last, a compassionate and patient friend with yourself.

Creating that friendship begins with emotional awareness.

Diagrams

These diagrams provide an overview of the book's most important ideas. We hope you find them helpful.

ESCAPING ———————————————— AVOIDING

TO EXTERNAL	EXTERNAL
CIRCUMSTANCES:	CIRCUMSTANCES:
Perfectionism	Boredom
Workaholism	Entitlement
Savior Searching	Impenetrable Optimism
Sex	Vacating
Idol Worship	Alcohol and Drugs
	Eating

STRATEGIES
FOR
NOT FEELING
PAINFUL EMOTIONS

CHANGING

EXTERNAL

CIRCUMSTANCES

Pleasing

Anger

Pass-through Effect

Power Struggles

Judging

Stress

WHEN POWER LEAVES IN . . .

Center	Fear and Doubt	Love and Trust
Seventh	Feel disconnected from nonphysical Universe	Feel connected with nonphysical Universe
Sixth	World appears cold and frightening—five-sensory perception only	See wisdom, compassion of Universe; meaning in every experience
Fifth	Constricted expression	Clear and powerful expression
Fourth	Fear love is impossible closed, defensive; people appear as objects	Feel connected to all of Life
Third	Anxious, feel unable to provide for self or defend self	Confident, relaxed
Second	Strong sexual craving; exploit others	Creative, celebrate Life
First	Earth does not feel like home, uncomfortable with your life.	At home and at ease on the Earth

THE POTENTIAL OF EACH ENERGY PATTERN

Pattern	Unhealed Perception	Healed Perception
Anger	I have every right to be angry.	I use the energy of anger to create a meaningful and creative life.
Workaholism	I am valuable because of what I do.	I am valuable just being.
Pass-through Effect	I deserve to indulge in every emotion I feel.	I feel my emotions and use them as \information about myself.
Perfectionism	I must make everything perfect.	I see that everything is perfect based on the wisdom of the choices that I have made.
Pleasing	I need to please others in order to feel whole.	I am whole and I naturally give to others as appropriate.
Vacating	I drift in fantasies and irrelevant activities.	I am grateful to be in the present moment.
Boredom	I find no meaning in external activities and people.	I see the value in everything and everyone, including myself.
Idol Worship	I am my role.	I am worthy as I am.
Optimism	I pretend that "All is well."	Everything that happens, including my painful emotions, is for the best.
Entitlement	I am superior and deserve everything I desire.	What I need is what I have.
Eating	I need nourishment from food that I am not getting from the Universe.	I gratefully receive nourishment from the Universe and I can truly nourish others.
Sex	My salvation is in my next sexual partner.	I am my own salvation.

Afterword

I F THIS BOOK WAS HELPFUL TO YOU, we recommend that you become a partner in the vision of Genesis: The Foundation for the Universal Human. Genesis is a nonprofit organization that provides tools, programs and events to help individuals create authentic power—the alignment of the personality with the soul. Partnership in the vision of Genesis: The Foundation for the Universal Human also provides a way for us to keep in touch and to share with you our future activities.

For more information, you can visit *www.universalhuman.org* or contact:

Genesis: The Foundation for the Universal Human
PO Box 339
Ashland OR 97520 USA
888 440 SOUL (7685)
541 482 8999 (outside USA)
genesis@universalhuman.org

You can also visit us at *www.zukav.com.*

Love,
Gary and Linda

Index

A

About the Authors

GARY ZUKAV is the author of *The Dancing Wu Li Masters: An Overview of the New Physics,* winner of the American Book Award for Science; *The Seat of the Soul,* the celebrated #1 bestseller in *The New York Times, USA Today, Los Angeles Times, Publishers Weekly,* and others; and the *New York Times* bestseller *Soul Stories.* His books have sold millions of copies and are published in sixteen languages. He is a graduate of Harvard and a former U.S. Army Special Forces (Green Beret) officer with Vietnam service.

LINDA FRANCIS is a cofounder of Genesis: The Foundation for the Universal Human, spiritual partner with Gary Zukav, and cocreator of *The Heart of the Soul.* Through Genesis, they offer retreats, programs, and other events supporting the creation of authentic power and the experience of spiritual partnership. They both live in Oregon.